Garden Work Centers

By the editorial staffs of
Sunset Books & Sunset Magazine

LANE BOOK COMPANY
MENLO PARK, CALIFORNIA

Foreword

Every gardener has a garden work center of sorts. Perhaps it is nothing more than a corner in the garage, with a few tools hung from the wall and a sack or two of fertilizer. Maybe it's the kitchen sink. Maybe it's just a shady spot on the patio, used from time to time as a place to pot a plant or divide a clump of dahlia tubers.

This is a book to help the home gardener who honestly enjoys his garden and wants a place out there where he can hang his hat and get to work. On these pages are ideas for gardens large and small—simple plant shelters, lathhouses of many sizes, lathed-over sideyards, greenhouses, coldframes, compost bins, storage units, and multi-purpose work centers with a little of everything. Most of the material has appeared in the pages of *Sunset Magazine* in recent years.

In the interests of presenting a large number of ideas for the garden builder, there has been no attempt to make this book an exhaustive, top-to-bottom study of any one subject. In the chapter on greenhouses, for instance, we have purposely avoided many scientific aspects. And we have not included the special techniques for hobbyists, such as orchid growers, who like to garden under glass. If this chapter suggests to you what type greenhouse might best suit your needs, then it has served its purpose. A reliable greenhouse manufacturer, with his knowledge of your area's weather and other considerations, should be consulted when you are ready to get down to brass tacks.

The two materials predominant in this book are wood lath and glass—tried and true for many years in garden structures the world over. But there are other kinds, some of them quite new (see page 96). The *Sunset* book, *How to Build Patio Roofs*, contains many examples of how to use these materials.

The talented gardener is not necessarily a talented builder. Because of this, you will find here and there throughout this book some do-it-yourself projects so elementary that even the most fumble-thumbed amateur can cover himself with glory. Turn to pages 22 and 23 for a few samples.

Once you start using your garden work center, you will wonder how you ever got along without it. You will garden with better system, and your flower beds will show it. There are many happy hours to be spent in the lathhouse or greenhouse or potting area—where you can almost hear the heartbeat of your garden.

Eleventh Printing September 1970

By the publishers of *Sunset* Books and *Sunset,* The Magazine of Western Living

Contents

Cover photograph by Ernest Braun (see page 56)
Title page photograph by Darrow M. Watt

Storage Wall

Water Source

Patio Table
and Work Bench

Lath Shelter

Heated
Frame

Growing Bed

Coldframe

Most of the plants *in this home's garden (beyond screens) were brought into the world in this home nursery. The coldframe was* *the first structure built and used. Growing bed, lath shelter, and heated frame came later. Donald Davis home, Bellevue, Wash.*

A gardening family can have its own "home nursery"

That quadrangle of workmanlike structures in the photograph at the top of this page is a home nursery, belonging to a family in Bellevue, Washington. Something like it, larger or smaller as you wish, could belong to any gardening family in the West.

The installation doesn't have to be this precise and well developed. The work could be done on the ground instead of on rigid tables and shelves. Infant plants could be started in a glass-topped fruit box instead of a coldframe, and young plants could mature in the shade of a tree instead of a lath shelter. However, this installation happens to be neat and sturdy enough to make a good demonstration of the whole idea.

Let's start from the top of this picture and move counter-clockwise around it to see what it is that makes a good home nursery work.

The potting and seeding table. That paved area between the house and the long lath shelter is the family's patio. Here, they eat, entertain, and rest. It's in view of the main garden. The table is their outdoor dining table. But since it is sturdy and easy to clean. it also serves as a

work bench on which to fill flats, make cuttings, and sow seeds to be grown in the home nursery. By mid-afternoon this table is in the shade of the house. This is important because new cuttings, being severed parts of a plant, can be set back or ruined by dehydration at the time you are preparing them.

The important feature is that the nursery is out of sight of the eating, entertaining, and loafing area. The lath shelter, gate, and storage wall screen it from view. Clay pots, wooden flats, uncoiled hoses, and wheelbarrows are not the prettiest things to look at day in and day out.

Some materials used in a home nursery can be downright unpleasant to have around—compost pits and fertilizer sacks, for instance. These are stored out of sight and out of smell, outside of the picture to the lower left.

The water source. Your nursery venture may fail without an easy, ready water supply close by your coldframe, the lath or tree shelter, and nursery beds. Many a well intended home nursery scheme has gone to pieces in operation because the water source was too remote to make it practical. Once the little plants begin to

form leaves of their own, their roots must seek water. And since their roots seek the water in a shallow, limited area, they depend on you to supply it. They do this to a much greater extent than the plants out in your garden, whose roots have ranged deep and wide. A hose from this water source can feed out to any part of

Here is *the heated frame with one sash open. Flats are resting on the heating cable. Cable is coiled over layer of sand*

the nursery area. Attached to a soaker or plastic tube sprinkler, it waters the lath shelter area (as shown in the right-hand photograph at the bottom of the page). The hose can also be used to wash down the patio paving.

The nursery paving. When you go through the gate into the nursery area, you step from a concrete paved entertaining and play area to a gravel-surfaced nursery area. Gravel can be soaked daily and have soil spilled on it often without it becoming unpleasant to walk on or needing any more maintenance than an occasional raking or hosing off.

The storage wall. Center left in the picture, you see the working side of the storage wall that screens the nursery from the rest of the garden. There are 4 shelves of stout 2-inch lumber on which pots are stacked and fertilizers and insecticides are stored from spring to fall. In winter, when there is little call for these products, they can be moved to the garage, basement, or other closed storage area.

The heated frame. That glass sash-covered box at far left, and its counterpart cold-frame at lower right, are where seeds and cuttings become plants. Such frames are indispensable if you are going to do much home nursery work. Their simplest equivalent is a box covered with a piece of glass. At the other extreme is a full-fledged greenhouse. One way or the other, seeds and cuttings need protection from the extremes of the weather. For this purpose, glass (or translucent plastic) is the best modifier of the elements that man has yet devised.

This particular frame has a thermostatically controlled heating cable coiled over its floor, with a heat-insulating sand layer between it and wet ground. The owners can use heat or not, depending on the season and their ideas of what might be proper for any particular propagating job.

The growing bed. Now, see that open rectangular bed at lower center. When plants are ready to go into the open soil, here is where you plant them out (the older garden books used to say, "Line them out in nursery rows"). These beds are the final growing spot for propagated plants—a place for plants that are too self-sufficient to need protection of lath or glass but not yet old enough for the garden, not yet presentable enough, or waiting until the main garden is made ready for them.

Some hardy or tough plants can be sown or started as cuttings right here. Others can go directly here from the coldframe. Others go the long way—from coldframe or heated frame (or greenhouse or glass-topped box) to under-lath to this open waiting or growing spot.

The coldframe. In the photograph's lower right, a double sash unheated frame stands in full sun. Because of the exposure, this frame is used only from late September until May when it takes full advantage of any available sunshine. If used in summer, keeping it watered becomes a major chore.

Easy-to-root cuttings of both evergreen and deciduous plants which are taken in fall are placed here and usually root by spring. Young seedlings and rooted cuttings started in the heated frame in spring and summer are placed in the cold-frame in fall, so they can receive good winter protection. Because of the cold-frame's sun exposure they develop into husky little plants that are ready to plant out in the nursery beds in the spring.

The lath shelter. Unless you have a big tree whose summer shaded area you can give over to flats and pots of little plants, a lath shelter is indispensable in the scheme of things. This family's lath shelter is the long, low, rectangular structure that runs from the middle of the picture to right center.

A lath shelter of this type can be a place of a hundred uses.

Once cuttings are rooted or seedlings are up in their flats under glass, you transplant them either to their spot in the garden or to open ground in a waiting area (growing bed). Or, if the little plants still need more care and growth before planting, transplant to flats or pots. And where is the best place to keep them? In this Bellevue garden, the coldframe is used through winter as an extra step, dictated by the winter weather and by the choice of the owner. If you sidestep the winter coldframe stage, or have the plants ready in spring, the lath shelter is ideal for the newly propagated plants in pots or flats. The plants would dry out too often if kept in full sun.

Newly rooted or sprouted shade plants, such as begonias, camellias, or rhododendrons, should definitely go under lath. Cuttings of many easy-to-start plants can be started under lath instead of glass. The lath keeps hot sun off them.

Open, cultivated soil under lath is a good place for starting hardwood cuttings.

A lath shelter will prove valuable again and again for keeping the surplus of any plants that require shade. Of course, if your lath shelter is big enough to walk under and sit under, you have a full-time growing place for shade plants there, but that is something else again.

Mist spray under lath? In the dry parts of the West, new or started cuttings and other young plants often need more moisture than a home gardener can supply with only a hose and syringe-spray attachment. Commercial growers have developed an automatic mist spray system, activated by a time clock, that holds great promise for home gardeners.

Supposing you live in such a climate and you have a lath structure like the one in this picture. You might go to a sprinkler system dealer or contractor and ask for a system to mist spray this structure. We can't say for sure just what kind of a system your dealer might lay out, but we can tell you what a Sacramento Valley dealer recommended gardeners use in a shelter in that climate. The structure is 5 feet wide and 12 feet long. A main line leading from a time clock runs down the center of the structure and is mounted just beneath the overhead and centered between the 2 sides. The line should contain 10 fogger heads, spaced 1 foot apart, and the first ones 1½ feet in from either end of the line.

The lowest cost would be about $70, itemized as follows: clock to activate the valve, about $20; electronic valve, $15; the 10 heads, at $2.50 each, totaling $25; pipe, $10.

You would set the clock to suit your watering schedule and climate.

About as simple *a greenhouse-substitute as you could devise. Cuttings rooting in soil. Jar holds moisture around the leaves*

Lath shelter *above is just a long, 12-inch high raised bed. The lath roof support posts also hold the bed's side pieces*

How to build lath shelters
Details to watch in building a lathhouse

Lath continues to be a year-in-and-year-out favorite of the garden builder. The lathhouse, the lathed-over side yard, the lath-and-glass combination—these and many other adaptations can be seen in gardens throughout the West.

The advantages of such structures are many. In dry climates, plant material requiring not only shade, but also moist air, can be safely grown. Humidity can be effectively increased by occasional sprinkling under a lathed area.

In many areas of the West where summer's sun is bright, the breaking of its rays through lath is beneficial to some of the most desirable summer plants, notably begonias and fuchsias. Also, where wind is a problem, the lath garden pays its way many times over.

Whether planted to full capacity, or used mainly as an outdoor living room, the lath garden, according to every owner we've met, is well worthwhile.

LATHHOUSE SIZE

The size of the lathhouse you build should be based on lath lengths. Laths are avail-able in 4-, 6-, and 8-foot lengths. (See diagram below.)

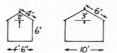

FOUNDATION

Although a creosoted redwood mud-sill makes a satisfactory foundation for a lathhouse, concrete is recommended for solidity and permanence, especially in large structures.

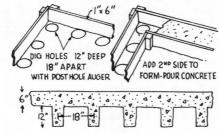

Concrete piles 18 inches deep insure a firmly anchored foundation. This is par-ticularly desirable in the case of lathhouses built on filled or sloping ground. Piers should go down through the fill well into solid ground.

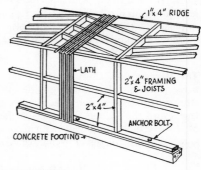

FRAMEWORK

According to experts, an invariable rule in lathhouse construction should be the pitched roof and the diagonal placement of the framing or the laths on the roof. Prevention of drip is the motive.

DRIP INSURANCE

The drip problem is best solved as shown (1) by placing the inter-rafter, nailing joists diagonally, and adding metal gutters (see illustration); (2) by placing the laths diagonally over greenhouse sash (drainage grooves could be cut on power saw). Use 2"x3" lumber. This method does not require inside gutter as in (1).

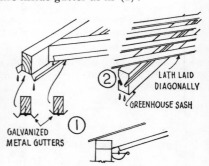

LATH PATTERNS

There are several interesting variations on the usual arrangement of laths. One features a combination of 3-foot squares alternately laid vertically and horizontally to form a checkerboard (see cut). Another variation makes use of laths laid vertically in a continuous line along the side of the structure for 6 feet, then places laths horizontally from top to bottom in the adjoin-

This lathhouse in the garden of Mr. and Mrs. Charles J. Dilke of Hillsborough, California, can be described most accurately as a lath conservatory. It is purely ornamental and includes no working space. The rich greens of the ferns and other plants, the soft light, and the redwood logs used around the beds are suggestive of cool forests. There is much color here in summer when the begonias and cinerarias bloom

ing 6-foot section. Still another combines both patterns.

ALTERNATING WIDTHS

The use of alternating widths of laths produces an especially pleasing effect. To achieve this, rip the necessary number of laths to half width. Spacing can be 1 to 1½ times the width of the lath.

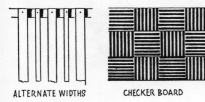

ALTERNATE WIDTHS   CHECKER BOARD

LIGHT CONTROL

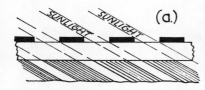

(a) Normal placement of laths—spaced one lath apart—cuts down morning and afternoon sunlight.

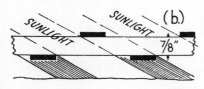

(b) With the same horizontal spacing and with alternating laths above and below the framework, a more even all-day light intensity is obtained. Noonday sunlight is the same in both cases.

ANT-PROOFING

Two methods of ant-proofing are shown here. In one, a space of 4 inches between the benches and the sides and ends of the lathhouse helps to exclude ants.

Added protection from ants, as well as from snails and slugs, is afforded by setting the supporting legs of the benches in water-filled containers (see cut).

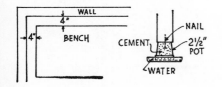

To keep the legs out of water, fill 2½-inch pots with cement, then place them in 8-inch porcelain rabbit feeders. Fill the feeders with water, and place the legs of the benches on the pots.

To prevent the legs from slipping off the pots, place a nail through the drainage hole of the pots, with the head inside the pot, and the pointed end projecting about ½

There is year-around enjoyment in this lathhouse belonging to Mr. and Mrs. C. M. Monroe of La Jolla, California.

Vines and an adjoining eugenia hedge exclude the prevailing west winds blowing in from the ocean. A pink and white color

inch through the drainage hole. Fill the pot with cement, then place a piece of wood or heavy cardboard over the cement. Turn the pot over so that the drainage end is upright, and allow the cement to harden. When the bench leg is placed on the concrete base, the nail penetrates the leg and holds it firmly in position.

BENCH CONSTRUCTION

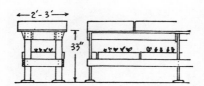

In the illustration above is a section of a lathhouse bench, showing the lower bench being used for cutting boxes or propagating cases. Strips of muslin, burlap, or canvas tacked to the lower section of the lathhouse at this point exclude drafts or excessive light.

BRICK-BOTTOMED BENCH

Here is a variation on the conventional cutting bench. Instead of using wood in the bottom, bricks are laid on 2"x2" redwood supports laid 8 inches apart (the length of a brick). No cement should be used between the bricks. The porosity of the

scheme is usually featured in this lathhouse. It is gay with azaleas in winter, and with tuberous begonias in summer. Primroses and cinerarias are the mainstay in spring. Moss-covered rocks, ferns, and vines help to create a cool, moist atmosphere

bricks and the small spaces between them permit excess water to drain off readily,

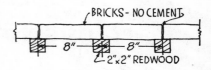

yet a certain amount of moisture is held by the bricks. In such a cutting bench, there is less danger from certain fungi that grow and flourish on wood.

TWO-PURPOSE LATHHOUSE

The Monroe lathhouse, shown in the photograph above, is a good example of the two-purpose structure. It is the logical lathhouse to be built by the gardener who has no greenhouse or separate potting-shed. The potting-bench is a good size and is well-equipped (it even includes a sink), yet it is in no way obtrusive, nor does it detract from the appearance of the lathhouse.

There is a pool on the left side, surrounded by mossy rocks and shade-loving plants. Above it is a gargoyle and a shell-shaped basin from which water drips to the pool. The lattice sides and ends of the lathhouse offer much more protection from winds and dry air than laths placed in the ordinary manner can provide.

Beams with lath overhead stretch from roof of house, left, to elevation sections above concrete wall, creating work area 60 feet long

Lath overhead makes a side yard usable

The photograph above shows how Designers Robert and Naomi Sommer converted a narrow side yard into usable garden work space. A long counter with storage bins below makes a potting center. The lath overhead shades the area and also screens the view from the neighbor's house on the right.

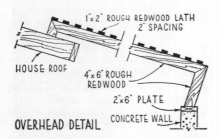

1″x 2″ ROUGH REDWOOD LATH
2″ SPACING

HOUSE ROOF

4″x 6″ ROUGH REDWOOD

2″x 6″ PLATE

CONCRETE WALL

OVERHEAD DETAIL

Tool storage locker built under the eave

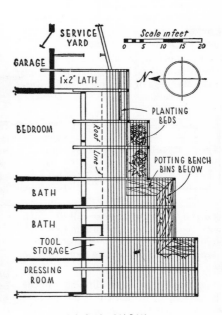

SERVICE YARD

GARAGE

1″x 2″ LATH

Scale in feet
0 5 10 15 20

N

BEDROOM

Roof Line

PLANTING BEDS

POTTING BENCH BINS BELOW

BATH

BATH

TOOL STORAGE

DRESSING ROOM

PLAN VIEW

Lathhouse for a large garden

Some lathhouses are for display, some for play, and some are built to work in. This example, in Bel-Air, Los Angeles, is a working lathhouse— designed by a working gardener. It serves as growing-up storage place for the plants destined for terraces and display beds, thereby ensuring continuous garden color the year around.

Here are soil bins for potting mixtures, pot storage, a shelf for plants which can take more sun than regular lath allows, space below for those liking less

Left. *House is seven feet high with 2 by 4 frame, 4 by 4 corners. There is room for large-scale soil mixing and compost bins in the fenced-in area*

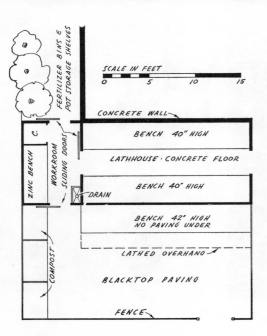

SCALE IN FEET
0   5   10   15

FERTILIZER BINS & POT STORAGE SHELVES

CONCRETE WALL

BENCH 40" HIGH

LATHHOUSE · CONCRETE FLOOR

ZINC BENCH C.

WORKROOM SLIDING DOORS

DRAIN

BENCH 40" HIGH

BENCH 42" HIGH NO PAVING UNDER

COMPOST

LATHED OVERHANG

BLACKTOP PAVING

FENCE

Benches are 40 inches high, 36 wide. Center space wide enough for wheelbarrow. Zinc-covered work table. "Toe-space" below counter

JAMES L. LAWRENCE

Garden shelter and display combined

HERE'S a man-made tree that can do most of the things for your garden that a growing tree, or a group of them, can do. Any object with height, width, and mass in some measure can be treated as a tree substitute in landscape design. But because Designer Ben Polk of San Francisco made this structure especially light in appearance, it is particularly eligible.

You can use it also as a lathhouse to protect tender plants, a place to show off prize blooms, and a garden shelter.

See the diagrams for construction details. The immediate area underfoot is covered with a concrete slab. The overhead covering is ordinary lath.

Graceful, light-appearing, this structure serves as tree substitute when garden is young

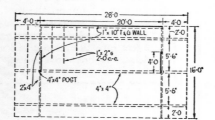

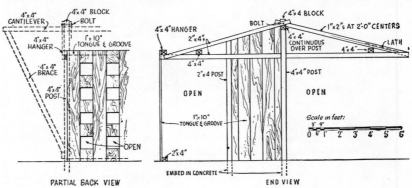

PARTIAL BACK VIEW

END VIEW

The light and airy quality of the structure is due in a large part to cantilevering of front roof section. Construction detail above

Corrugated aluminum roof edge is painted yellow; laths are stained brown. Lath on roof should be laid perpendicular to the path of the sun. Overhang casts little shadow

Bins are balanced so that they are self closing but can be held open for filling by inserting peg. Step shelves above bins are convenient. Hanging baskets out of way

For an average-sized garden

ALL TOO OFTEN, a garden lath house is an unsightly work shed kept out of sight behind a planting screen or garden fence. Obviously, it would be far more desirable to have a pleasant work-space in the garden where potting shelves and peat, sand, and loam bins would be easy to get to. Here is one designed by Landscape Architects Katy and Paul Steinmetz and shown at the Marin County, California, Art and Garden Show.

This structure was designed for gardeners whose activities are confined to average-sized city lots. It is attractive enough to be brought into the yard where it is more convenient to use.

While it was not intended to be anything more than a pleasant and efficient work-space, this lath house might be enlarged to serve almost any garden purpose. For example, if the roof were extended, it could be used as an outdoor dining shelter. Construction hints: While 2-by-4 joists are not necessary to support the roof, use them to assure ample support for hanging baskets. Use redwood for corner posts; set them 2 feet into the ground and creosote to at least 3 inches above grade.

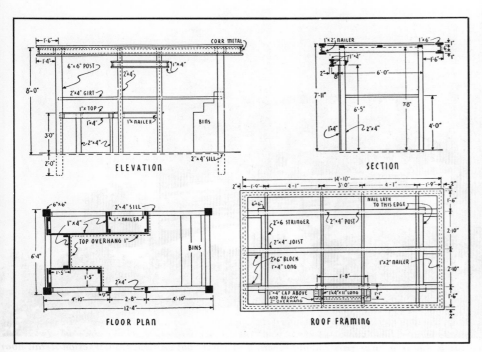

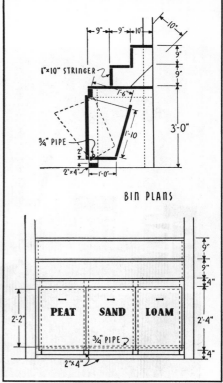

WILLIAM C. APLIN

Pleasant to work in ... and look into

THE OWNER of this lathhouse, Miss Margaret Blaney of Montecito, California, originally consulted an architect for the purpose of remodeling a bedroom so that it would open directly into the garden. When estimated costs ran higher than expected, Landscape Designer R. R. Brimer of Santa Barbara was asked to design a lathhouse which would be placed so that it could be seen from all rooms except the kitchen. The result was a structure which includes every practical feature necessary to satisfy the most fastidious gardener, yet at the same time one which is an attractive addition to the outdoor living area.

Lathhouse of redwood, 15 by 30 feet, hollow tile foundation. Left end joins fence, workshop at right. Stained with brown shingle oil

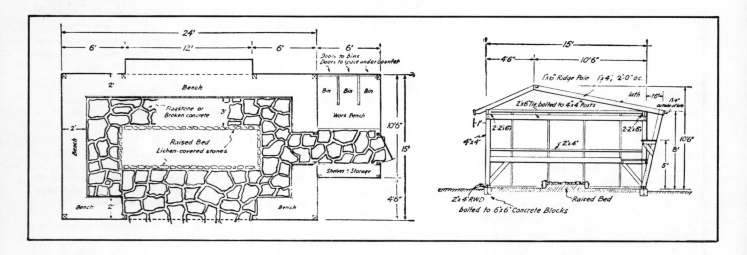

Bench at right is filled with expanded mica; other benches have slatted bottoms. Potting shed in rear has solid roof, three storage bins with outside openings. Sloping shelf above work bench holds small tools. Flagstone floor

Ramp leading from potting shed into garden makes it easy to handle a wheelbarrow. Decorative note in planted hollow tile on either side

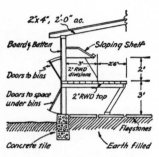

Upper openings with metal sides for un-loading potting materials. Lower section is for pots. Note sloping side of lathhouse

Begonia shelter and garden work center. Mist spray and split bamboo supplement lath and approximate a begonia climate. Plants are started here, then moved to shaded terrace when in bloom. Lath roof is made by extending garage rafters. Paving is asphalt

Lath lean-to

HERE'S a compact lath lean-to that serves a double purpose. It provides potting bench and storage space for garden staples. It also solves a climate problem for a begonia grower in a hot, dry area unsuited to the moisture-loving plant.

The lean-to occupies space eight feet wide between the garage and the property line in Dr. and Mrs. Verne Ross' garden in Stockton, California. Landscape Architect Douglas Baylis of San Francisco designed it for Mrs. Ross.

If you take the lean-to apart, you find it is made of three versatile units—a work and storage bench, a flower stand, and an overhead panel of lath. Each unit has its own possibilities for garden use.

pot soil on such a work bench, substitute two-inch lumber for the one-inch stock. Bench is wide enough for a flat.

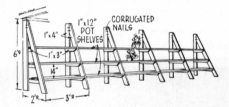

The triangle-framed pot shelves could serve equally well as a free-standing garden partition—with seasonal color changes to brighten the scene. Or you might use the stand as a plant display unit against a fence, garage, lathhouse, or greenhouse.

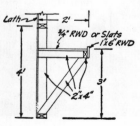

Outward sloping side of lathhouse creates extra space, a feeling of depth, and an interesting setting for the potted plants

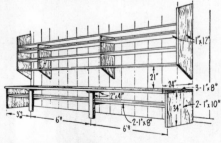

The bench unit is a simply constructed series of shelves which you might attach to garage, barbecue shelter, or lathhouse. With just a minimum of overhead protection, it would become a modified work center that the average gardener could use the year around. If you like to mix your

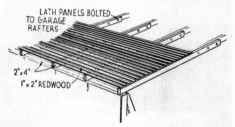

The lath roof is made of 1 by 2 redwood, nailed directly to the rafters. As a separate lath panel, it makes an excellent building unit for garden structures of almost any shape and size, and can be placed to advantage in nearly any garden that wants to utilize available space.

Lathhouse on a hillside

Lathhouse roof as seen from the path above which follows slope contour. Left, retaining wall breaks prevailing north wind, supports terrace above. Vegetables are at left of path

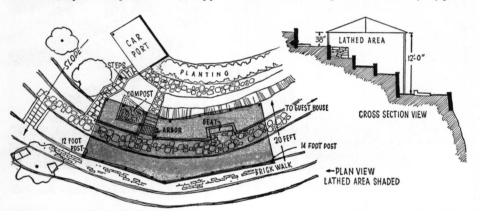

JERRY ANSON

Inside the lathhouse, where azaleas, camellias, fuchsias, begonias are grown successfully

IN CLIMATES that are hot and windy in summer, and in gardens where there are no large trees to cast shade, lath comes to the rescue of the gardener who wants to grow successfully plants that demand shade. Through the use of a lath covering over a large part of their terraced, hillside garden, the Earl S. Webbs of San Bernardino, California, achieved maximum planting space and have been able to grow camellias, azaleas, and fuchsias in a section generally considered unfriendly to shade-loving plants.

The lath roof shown here, which is 65 feet long and spans 21 feet, covers a path and planting beds that follow the contour of the slope. Supporting posts on three levels are four by four-inch redwood with two by four-inch braces. All four by four-inch members are set on cement blocks, and are secured with spikes driven into the bottom of the posts, with the other end imbedded in the cement at the time of pouring it.

Three coats of paint were applied to all surfaces of the wood before the structure was built. The blue-green color blends beautifully with the various greens of foliage, and also with the sky. At times, the roof seems so light and airy and so much a part of the sky that it appears to be floating in space.

An overhead sprinkling system, consisting of two rows of one-half-inch pipe, runs the entire length of the structure. To provide adequate pressure, three-quarter-inch pipe has been used from the take-off to the two valves controlling the sprinkling system. Sprinkler heads are of the regular lathhouse spray type. Heads producing a fine, mist-like spray—the type used on vegetable stands—proved unsatisfactory, because the alkali in the water frequently plugged the tiny openings in the spray heads.

Mr. Webb also has found that one-inch spacings between the laths do not provide adequate shade during the warmest weather. Therefore, he plans to cover the entire lath roof with mesh netting.

On the south side of the lath shelter, a Concord grapevine and large hibiscus provide shade for smaller plants. The north side is bounded by a retaining wall made of native rock from a nearby canyon.

Although camellias, azaleas, begonias, and hardy orchids are among the shade plants grown by the Webbs, fuchsias are their main interest. Mr. Webb's method of propagating fuchsias is so successful that it is worth passing on here as a tip to other gardeners who grow these plants.

Cuttings two inches long are made from small, succulent shoots growing off the main stem, and which usually are removed, in any case. Cuttings are inserted into a sandy peat mixture within five minutes after they are taken from the plant. In addition to working with speed, Mr. Webb is particularly careful to keep the cuttings moist. Once they dry out, they are almost sure to be lost.

Fence and gate at left are made of lath material to match the plant shelter. Notice how lathhouse and greenhouse share one wall

Lath-and-glass combination

The shed roof of this greenhouse makes it possible to use clerestory windows for high ventilation. Thus there is no need to cut other openings in the ceiling, and the roof itself can more easily be made leakproof. The flat roof of the lathhouse fits just under the clerestory window level. Design: Waldemar C. Eller. Owner: Mrs. Mandana Beckner, Bel-Air, California.

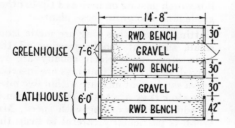

Glass and lath shelters get morning sun, but are shaded in afternoon by the oak trees

Lathhouse and greenhouse *create sitting area sheltered from wind and summer afternoon sun, yet receives full winter sun*

Lathhouse, car port, greenhouse . . . all in one

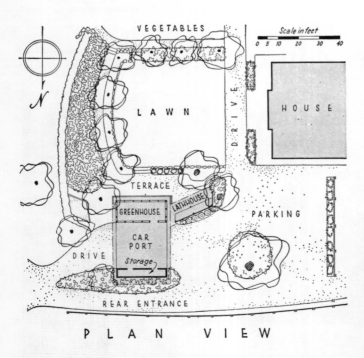

The plan view *shows how well the car port, greenhouse, and lathhouse have been integrated into the over-all plan and points up their accessibility from the house, garden, and parking area*

By attaching a greenhouse and lathhouse to an existing car port, Architect William Simrell got the following worthwhile results at his home in Los Altos, California:

One compact unit instead of several scattered buildings.

A windbreak for the lawn area in front of the house—used regularly for relaxing and play.

An additional sitting area (a terrace in front of the greenhouse and lathhouse.)

White horizontal *trellis across car port eave ties into greenhouse and lathhouse on the right and into storage room on the left*

In warm summer weather, the south and west sides of the greenhouse are shaded with bamboo blinds hung from the eaves

A pleasant approach to the car port.

An orderly as well as interesting enclosure on one side of the parking area.

The greenhouse actually looks more like a glassed-in garden room, although it serves all the conventional purposes of a greenhouse. It is used for starting seeds of flowers and vegetables, for growing potted plants, and for carrying tender material through the winter months. Potting soil, peat, sand, and fertilizers are stored under the benches, and there is also ample room for stacking empty pots and flats.

Stock 4 by 5-foot sashes, costing approximately $12 each, are used in the greenhouse. Grooves on the sides of each sash carry off rain and prevent it from entering cracks between the sashes.

The roof is covered with plastic-dipped screen in 4-foot-wide strips overlapping 4 inches. The screen is fastened down with redwood 1 by 2-inch battens. Roof pitch is $\frac{1}{2}$ inch to 12 inches. (Where rainfall is heavier, pitch should be at least 1 inch to 12 inches.) Since the adjoining car port roof slopes in the opposite direction, it delivers very little, if any, water onto the greenhouse.

The outer wall of concrete blocks is topped with board fence, in front of raw cut bank

For difficult areas

Construction of this lath shelter is simple. The 2 by 4 stringer which runs along the wall over the windows was nailed to the house studs. The posts are 4 by 4's. The beams are 4 by 8's. Rafters are 2 by 4's

Both of these lath shelters fill the awkward area between the hillside house and the raw bank behind it.

The Herman Janetzkys of Northridge, California, had only 10 feet between the rear wall of the house and a raw cut bank (see above). But by filling the space with rich topsoil and covering it with lath, they made it into an ideal shelter for shade and humidity loving plants ordinarily foreign to the warm, dry climate of the San Fernando Valley. A pipe runs along the rafters to supply a mist spray.

The rear windows of the Mark Musgrave home in La Mesa, California (shown at left), looked out on a rocky cut only five feet away, until a simple lath shelter turned the strip into a living green wall with a year-around flower display.

Bird nest fern, maidenhair fern, tuberous begonias give summer color. Cymbidiums, camellias give winter color.

Before planning such a structure, it is a good idea to check building codes so you will know how close you may build to your property line.

Greenhouse *entered from car port. Lathhouse has 1 by 2-inch lath on roof, $\frac{1}{2}$ by 2-inch lath on sides; and 2 by 4 stringers*

LATH HOUSE

PATIO ROOF

GARDEN
WORK CENTER

GARAGE

HOUSE

1 *Overhead view shows how separate parts of this garden structure fit together. House, left and lower right, forms two walls of the garden "room." Work center and lathhouse,* *upper left, form third wall. Fourth side is open. Ceiling of garden room is partly sky, partly the lofty, sloping patio roof, upper right. Roof shades approximately half the patio*

Lathhouse, patio, and garden work center

3 *Raised bed is planted with golden bamboo, holly fern, aucuba. Instead of lath, designer used 1 by 3 boards, 1-inch spacing*

4 *Fence section conceals disorder of potting center from patio. Bench equipped with second hand kitchen sink*

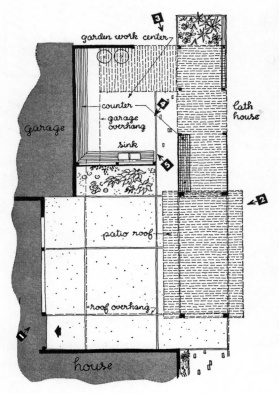

PLAN: *Small numbers show angles from which each photograph was made. Note how roof overhangs provide weather protection on two sides. For views through lathhouse, see next page*

2 *Facing south, this is year-around warm patio, usable even on winter days for barbecuing, play, entertaining. Furnishings include Navy surplus ship's table, small barbecue*

. . . designed as a unit . . . joined to the house

5 *Work center has concrete floor, 26 feet of heavy duty counter. Peat, sand, fertilizers stored under counter, tools on wall*

The outdoor structures pictured here occupy a space 21 by 43 feet where house and car port make an ell.

Into this space an open 21 by 23-foot patio, a small lathhouse, and a generous 13 by 23-foot work center fit together neatly.

As you study the photographs, note the following attributes of the plan:

1. The patio roof is located away from the house. While a roof linked directly to the house is more common, a separate roof screens out less of the welcome winter sun.

2. The patio roof is lofty, a sunshade floating 10 to 12 feet over your head.

3. The patio roof's line repeats the roof line of the house. As a result the one seems to belong to the other.

4. The garden work center is directly alongside the patio and lathhouse. Yet the disorder of tools, pots, and gardener's paraphernalia can't be seen from the patio.

5. The lathhouse is a cool hallway off the patio. It serves as a showcase for plants, decorating the patio, and adding to its cool garden atmosphere.

6. All three units—patio, lathhouse, garden work center—were designed and built as a unit, and joined directly to the main house structure. The result is economy in space and in cost.

To see how the approach Landscape Architect Douglas Baylis used here can apply in other situations, turn the page.

How to adapt the lathhouse-patio-work center plan to different situations

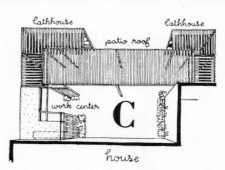

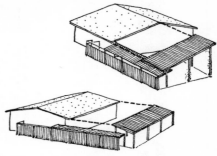

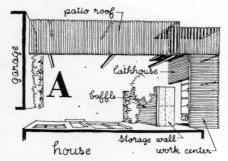

How this plan adapts itself to different garden situations . . .

Case A: Here the garage is at the rear of the house. Lathhouse and work center are built opposite the garage. Patio roof joins the two, creating an open garden room, part in the sun, part shaded by the patio roof.

Case B: On a narrow lot, the garden work center goes beside the house, completely out of sight from the patio. Lathhouse forms one wall of the patio. Opposite side is open to the garden.

Case C: On a wider lot, or where the house forms an ell, you can build the lathhouse in two sections, one on either side of the patio roof. In sketch at right, "working" lathhouse at left is next to garden work center, "display" lathhouse at right goes against the house.

If yours is a one story gable roofed house, your patio roof can repeat either of two roof lines (see sketches at right). If your

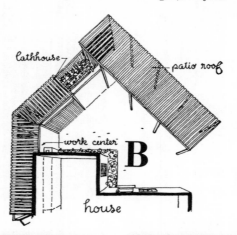

roof line is complicated, a flat roof is usually the wisest choice.

If your indoor floor level is well above ground level, so much the better. With roof level remaining the same and floor level dropping, your garden room will be

loftier and more open than any indoor room, as it should be. For a good example of this, and for many other ideas for garden room overheads, see the *Sunset* book, *How to Build Patio Roofs.*

Looking through lathhouse *toward house, down a long and cool garden corridor. Roofed walk (beyond patio in background) continues around house, repeats red brick paving of lathhouse*

Looking toward lathhouse, *the patio roof appears to float in space, anchored by its 6 by 6 supporting posts. Succulent planting, lower left. Vines in redwood boxes trained up posts*

Low level plant shelter

Movable lath structure *pulls out to shade plants, slides back for easy storage. Ends, on hinges, are dropped to support the top*

As the sun travels its course from spring to fall, it is apt to turn a location that is cool and moist during the winter and spring into a hot spot in summer and fall. This reversal of form creates a tough problem for the shade-plant gardener.

Mr. and Mrs. Richard C. Kern of Woodside, California, faced just such a problem when they wanted to use cinerarias for color outside a southeast window.

Their solution was this sliding lath structure, which can be pulled out over the plants during the sunny morning hours and pushed back during the rest of the day to show off the blossoms.

Similar structure might be used to protect newly rooted cuttings or seedlings. Covered with cloth or paper, it could be used to protect tender plants from killing frosts at night.

ROBERT COX

When not in use *lath is slid in under living room where it is suspended on metal channels secured to beam under floor*

Variety of containers *on shelf between posts is the result of patient shopping in old Japanese nurseries and pottery stores. Post construction gives the structure a light, airy feeling. Four 8 by 2 by 2's are bolted to 3 by 6's and 2 by 4's overhead*

A "stage" for bonsai

A bonsai collection actually dictated this landscape plan. Even before they moved into their Reseda, California, home, the Sterling Leach family were experienced practitioners of bonsai, the age-old Japanese art of growing living dwarfed trees in small containers.

Their first need was a lathhouse and display area for the bonsai. A lath overhead with lath running north and south that would give 40 to 50 per cent shade was just right for protection from the San Fernando Valley's summer sun. The shelter is 36 by 24 feet; 36-foot-long beams are 3 by 6's, and the 24-foot rafters are 2 by 4's. Rafters were spaced on 2-foot centers so that regular 4-foot lath could be used without waste.

Across the yard, another overhead extends from the living-dining area of the house. A tree, growing next to the house, is beginning to grow up through the opening that was left for it. The shelter extends along side of garage (hidden by trees).

Quick shade for plants . . . or people

Somewhere in every garden, as soon as the weather turns warm, quick shade for plants or people is usually needed. You may feel that you need such shade only for one or two summers—until trees have grown up or a permanent structure can be constructed. But there is no reason why an easily made shade structure cannot become a permanent part of your garden, provided it is well designed and soundly built. Here are seven structures that are easy to install; all give light, airy shade.

Most wood construction should be stained or painted before final installation. Aluminum tubing may be painted to cut the glare in hot, dry areas, but it can be left to weather naturally, since it is made to resist the elements. Before you decide what kind of supporting frame to use, choose the type of material you want overhead, since this material will determine spacing, and often size, of the overhead members.

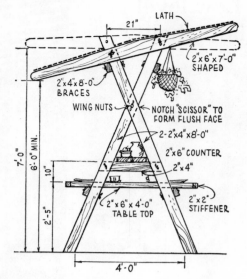

Plant display with an X-frame...

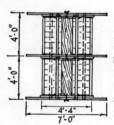

Plant display stand to protect shade loving plants on a warm terrace. Lath overhead of 1 by 2-inch wood strips, covered by reed or split bamboo shade, to cut afternoon sun, breeze. Paint 2 by 4-inch scissor frame and 2 by 6-inch overhead member a bright color to contrast with natural reed color.

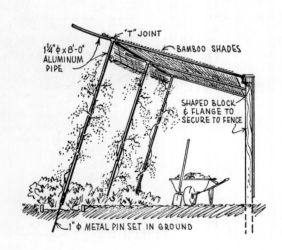

On an aluminum pipe frame...

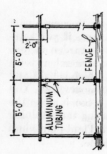

Aluminum pipe frame forms a lightweight support for shrimp netting or reeds along the house wall. Structure is made of pipe straps, horizontal pipe supports bolted to the frame, and metal pins set into the ground. T-joint construction permits the use of tubing without extra cutting or threading to complete the joint. Aluminum may be etched easily to make a base for paint in bright color.

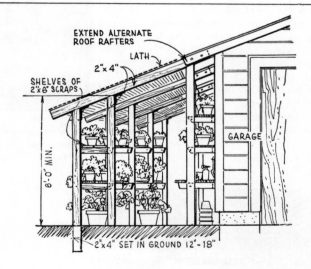

An extension of the rafters...

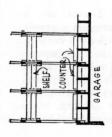

A simple shelter for plants, or a work space, may be made from 2 by 6-inch rafters bolted to existing rafters of the garage roof. And waste space along a side of an existing garage is utilized. Rafters should be spaced to match the roof members but should not be more than 32 inches apart. Full 1 by 2-inch lath is superior to thinner wood strips. Make shelves 1 inch thick for maximum support.

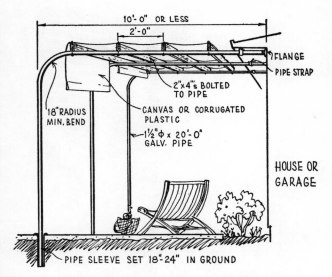

Wood rafters on a steel pipe frame...

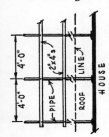

Temporary shade support made from standard 21-foot length of pipe in 1¼ or 1½-inch diameter; pipe can be bent in the middle before delivery. Support is slipped into pipe sleeve at ground level; flange is below the eave. Bolt 2 by 4-inch rafters to the frame for easy dismounting. Overhead can be canvas, net, or reed matting.

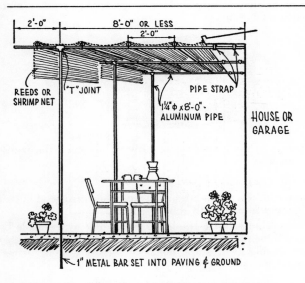

Aluminum tubes with a T-joint...

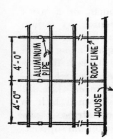

Two aluminum tubes, a T-joint, and a flange form one of the simplest supports for overhead bamboo shades yet devised. Aluminum is an ideal metal for supporting plants in hot inland valleys, since it does not heat excessively. The supports are spaced 36 inches apart to prevent the overhead material from sagging; wires may be used to secure the material to the pipe supports.

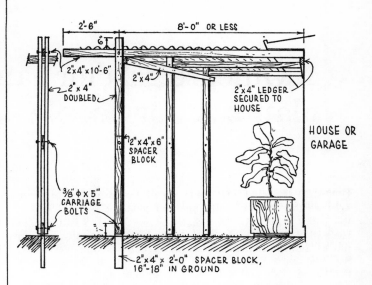

Shade shelter with built-up posts...

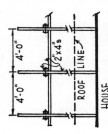

Simple, distinctive garden structure is made with built-up post of 2 by 4-inch members, spaced apart to receive overhead rafters and the wood pin that goes into the ground. Overhead shade may be lightweight corrugated asbestos board or corrugated plastic. Fasten to the rafters by screws for easy dismounting.

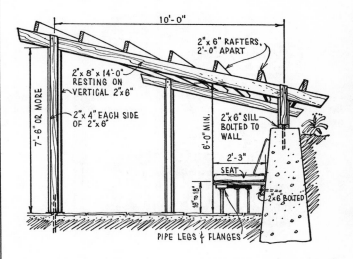

Wood trellis anchored to a wall...

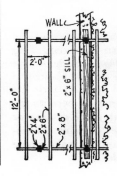

Concrete retaining walls can become a part of a pleasant sitting terrace if you integrate them properly into a garden shelter. In this design simple wood members form the trellis construction, which is light and airy in contrast to the masonry wall. You can build a seatwall or a couch along the low side of the arbor, using the retaining wall as the back support. Plant light vines for overhead summer shade.

Multi-use garden panels

With them you can build almost any garden structure

CONSIDER what you could do in the garden with these light-weight, sturdily built, modular panels.

Each is a 3 by 6-foot rectangle—giving you a 3-foot square basic unit to play with. Two panels laid horizontally, one on top of another, equal the height of one standing vertically. Set in a simple frame, they make a fence that's both a practical windbreak and attractive in design.

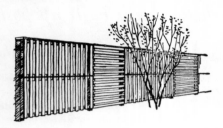

You can use the panels singly as a cover for lath frame or coldframe, or to protect flats of young seedlings.

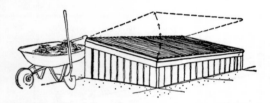

. . . or as an eyebrow-like projection on a fence to shade your favorite plants. If you hinge them, you can fold them back against the fence in winter.

The panels will combine to make shelters large and small—either for plant protection or for outdoor living. They make natural extensions to any room, make the addition of a lath type shelter to an existing structure an easy one.

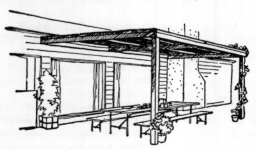

Each panel weighs about 25 pounds—light enough for a man to handle. You can build them yourself or buy them ready-made at a lumber yard.

They are as adaptable to modern design as they are to a more conventional lathhouse.

On the next three pages are more ways in which the panels might be used.

HOW TO MAKE THE PANELS

The frame for the panels is made of 2 by 2-inch redwood butted together and secured with galvanized nails.

Corners are braced with triangular pieces of 2 by 4—made by cutting a 4-inch piece of 2 by 4 diagonally. Other and probably cleaner bracing devices are: metal corner irons, angle braces, and metal straps.

Instead of standard lathhouse lath, panels call for 1 by 2-inch redwood. This lumber is stronger, won't sag and curl, and it looks better. Alternate possibilities are redwood lath (3/8 by 2 inches) or redwood battens (3/8 by 3 5/8 inches).

For variety, you can fill in some of your panels with glass, canvas, or plastic instead of lath.

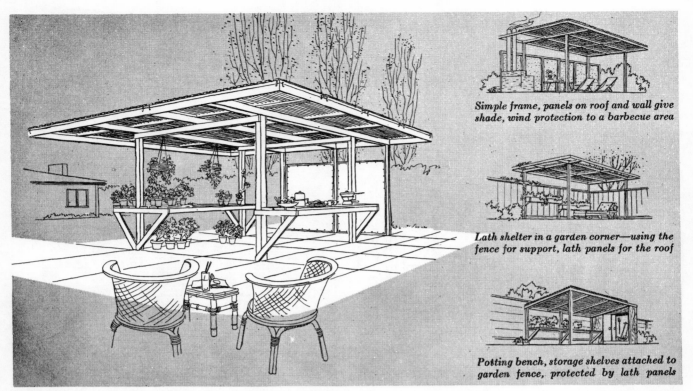

Simple frame, panels on roof and wall give shade, wind protection to a barbecue area

Lath shelter in a garden corner—using the fence for support, lath panels for the roof

Potting bench, storage shelves attached to garden fence, protected by lath panels

Garden work center with living space as by-product. Wide overhang protects outside plant shelves, keeps display space out of working space. Bench on right doubles as table for outdoor dining. Panels make it flexible, easy to expand, easy to change

For glass panels, the 2 by 2's will have to be rabbeted to hold the glass. An additional 2 by 2, with both edges rabbeted, will provide center support and make possible the use of standard greenhouse glass. Glass can be set in like shingles, held in place with standard glazing nails and staples.

The glass panels won't make a leak-proof roof. If you want your roof rain-tight, don't use the panels.

Canvas panels need a 2 by 2 cross-brace to prevent bowing in of the frame's 2 by 2's.

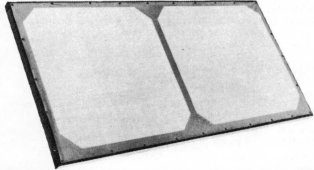

Use natural canvas; it comes in a 36-inch width. Cut it about ¾-inch wide on all edges, and fold this edge underneath so that the canvas forms its own washer. Tack it down with galvanized roofing nails. Start tacking in the center, and work toward the edges. If you want color, paint the canvas with a regular canvas paint; or you can use factory-painted canvas.

Instead of canvas, you may prefer to use woven plastic shade cloth (see page 96). Staple the cloth to the frame. You don't have to turn under the edges. For a more finished appearance, you can cover the stapled edges with a strip of standard window stop.

THE SUPPORTING FRAMEWORK

Build the skeleton framework to fit the panels—basing it on the 3-foot square. Use 4 by 4's for uprights, 2 by 4's for rafters and other horizontal members. Work it out so lath will run north and south.

Best height is 7 feet—obtained by framing in the bottom of your structure with a 2 by 12, setting the panels on top of it. An alternative is to set a vertical panel on top of a horizontal one—for a nine-foot height.

You don't need a solid concrete foundation. Easiest way to secure your structure to the ground is to stand your 4 by 4 uprights in concrete-filled holes. Soak the posts in a pentachlorophenol wood preservative before you set them in place. Concrete piers would be a second choice—but weaker.

Vertical posts provide support for work benches and pot shelves as shown in the flat-roofed shelter at the top of the page.

More ideas for multi-use garden panels:

Add them to a triangle frame . . .

Lean-to plant shelter with potting bench, starting racks, work space. Tools, supplies in garage; door to garage is wheelbarrow width. Structure uses 4 triangle frames, 9 panels for the roof

A 16 by 24-foot lathhouse—made by facing sets of triangular frames toward each other, roofing with panels. Shelves, bench, sit in framing, with room for center bench, wide aisles both sides

Panels fill in top and sides of this triangle frame—making a versatile unit you can lean against a building or stand in the garden by itself. Or you can lean one against another to make a full-sized lathhouse.

Used by itself, as a garden flower stand, it can add a splash of color wherever it's placed. To make it, use two of the lean-to frames to support two lath roof panels.

Or use two of the flower stands together for close-up display of your favorite miniature plants.

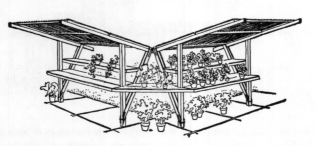

As a lean-to, it's an easy-to-attach addition to garage, house, fence, or another garden structure.

When the frames are used to make a hip-roofed lathhouse (drawing above), panels fit roof, sides, and ends of the triangular frames. Unfilled sections where panels do not fit can be filled with lath or plastic screen.

With this same hip-roofed structure you can combine lathhouse and greenhouse under one roof.

Wall of plastic screen cuts the house in half — glass panels make the roof and walls on one side, lath panels on the other.

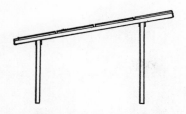

. . . or use them with a shed roof

A multi-purpose outdoor room—with work bench, shelves, and a bird-proof plant shelter for the gardener; a hanging display garden for the plant specialist in the family, entertaining space for parties; breezeway, shade, garden view for all. Minimum structure, minimum enclosure keep it a light, airy part of garden. As a kitchen extension, it makes outdoor eating easy

How you use this shed-roof frame depends upon how you've come to use your garden. Here are just a few of the possibilities:

The frame is easily made into an outdoor living room—by adding a barbecue pit, using lath panels for the roof, canvas panels for color and wind protection.

If you need your frame for plant protection, and summer shade is your only requirement, use lath panels on the roof alone to make a simple overhead shelter. For more protection, close in the sides and the ends with lath. The frame is designed so that panel-size units will close all but a triangular space below the roof. Close this in with plastic screen, lath, or glass.

If cold north winds bite through the lath in winter, place canvas or plastic screen panels in the path of the wind—or use a roll-down piece of canvas that you can drop in the winter, keep up in the summer.

With a glass roof and lath sides, you have a semi-greenhouse in which you can at least sample some of the fun of gardening under glass .

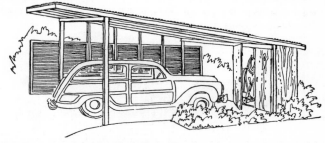

However you use the shelter, it can double as a car port either for your own or a guest's car—if it's accessible from your driveway and you provide means for clearing the floor area.

Or with canvas panels to wall in dressing rooms and with lath overhead, it can make a fine pool-side cabana.

You can hang a small-space work unit on your fence

Border of lath makes it possible to raise camellias, azaleas, and other shade plants

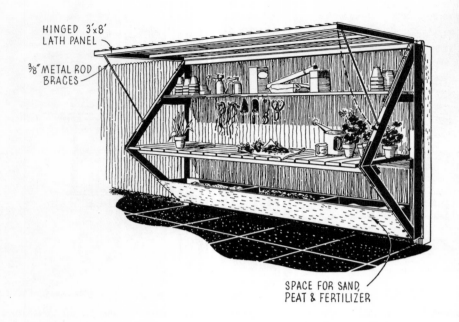

HINGED 3'x8' LATH PANEL

⅜" METAL ROD BRACES

SPACE FOR SAND, PEAT & FERTILIZER

Temporary lath shade

A lath overhang built along the top of a high fence provides quick shade. This is also a good device to use when putting in shade trees. When trees are grown enough to protect shade-loving plant material underneath, the lath can be removed. Owners: Mr. and Mrs. Albert R. Moore, San Marino, California.

HERE IS one way to save space in building a garden work center. With posts set in concrete and angle bracing as shown, the fence will carry all the work space you need.

In working out the structure, consideration was given the gardener who likes company when he's puttering. And who thinks that a well-arranged workshop rates a place in the outdoor living room.

Two variations in use are shown here.

How you use the work center, whether you will use lath or glass on drop panel will depend, of course, on how you garden. With a glass panel or a panel covered with plastic screen, a gardener can use the unit for the same purpose that a greenhouse serves when sowing seeds or making cuttings. If the unit is used to store items that should be protected from the weather, a glass or a screen panel should be used and the space enclosed above the top shelf.

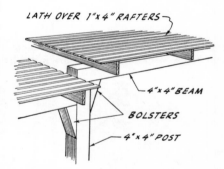

LATH OVER 1"x4" RAFTERS

4"x4" BEAM

BOLSTERS

4"x4" POST

Panels can change levels on a sloping site

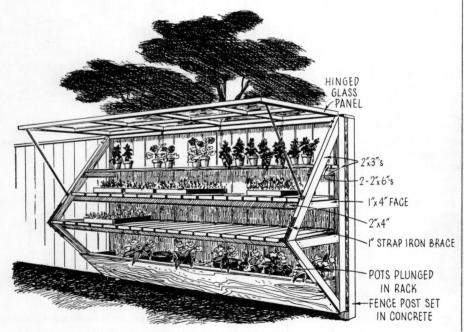

HINGED GLASS PANEL

2"x3"s

2-2"x6"s

1"x4" FACE

2"x4"

1" STRAP IRON BRACE

POTS PLUNGED IN RACK

FENCE POST SET IN CONCRETE

Diagonal 2½ by 1¾-inch brace helps to support beam. The slats are ½ by ⅜-inch

Lathhouse on wheels

Follow the seasons around your garden

A LATHHOUSE which can be moved from one place to another in the garden has some advantages over a stationary lathhouse. It can be kept in the sun as the seasons change. It can be moved to any part of the garden to make potting or other work easier. It can be moved out of sight when not in use.

The portable lathhouse shown here was designed by Hi Sibley of Nuevo, California, for use both as a lathhouse and as a potting bench. Although its construction requires some knowledge of carpentry, it is essentially a hammer and saw project.

The structure can be turned easily by lifting with the handles and pivoting on the front wheels. Brass bushing in the wheels could be left out for simplicity in construction, but they reduce friction, making it easier to roll the structure.

Semi-pneumatic, rubber-tired wheels similar to those on wheelbarrows may be used in place of wood wheels. Six-inch wheels may be obtained very reasonably.

General over-all dimensions are given in the diagrams below. Build the frame by following these dimensions and fit the intermediate parts after you have made your own measurements.

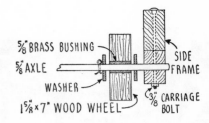

Wheel detail using wood wheel. If pneumatic, wheels would need ½-inch axle. Ball bearings would make moving easier

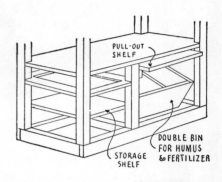

Redwood used for frame. Waterproof plywood used for top counter, storage shelf

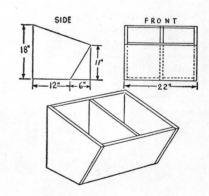

Plan calls for stationary double bin, but it could be hinged or made to pull forward

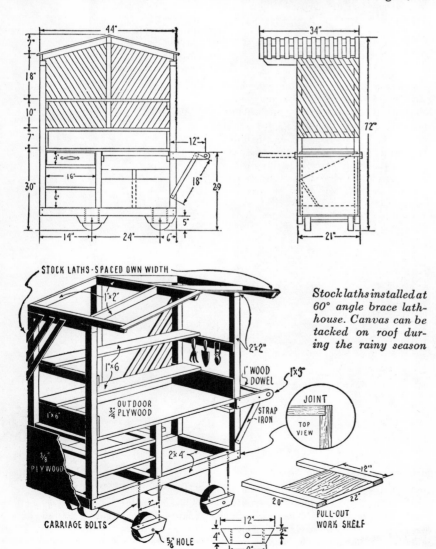

Stock laths installed at 60° angle brace lathhouse. Canvas can be tacked on roof during the rainy season

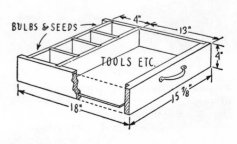

Bottom of drawer is ¼-inch plywood. Wood in lathhouse coated with linseed oil

When you garden under glass . . . spring

As gardens change to take on the function of an outdoor living room, greenhouse design becomes more important. No longer is it necessary to settle for the old standard small-paned glass box. In recent years, many gardeners have come to realize that a greenhouse should be a harmonious part of the total garden design.

Look at the inviting garden house pictured here. Note its materials—natural wood, glass, red brick. Note its combination of gable and flat roof, its half-octagonal show window for the display of the gardener's favorites. In scale, proportion,

materials, this small structure seems properly at home in its garden setting.

This is shelter for people as well as for plants. On cool spring or fall days it invites you to step inside, sniff the fragrance of flowers, work at the counters or relax on the bench, as you wish.

comes earlier . . . and summer lingers . . .

On these 26 pages . . . glasshouses, greenhouses, and coldframes for the part-time gardener and the all-out hobbyist. Some are large, many quite small . . . a few are actually a part of the house

When you place glass or a glass substitute over a plant, you give the plant a new little world of its own. Like the world outside, this glass enclosed world is lighted and heated by the sun, but it is a warmer and safer place on cold days or frosty nights. Within this shelter spring comes earlier **and** summer stays longer.

When you add artificial heat and control the humidity within this glass enclosure, you create a world without seasons. You can transplant the tropics to the northern

Viewed from overhead, this greenhouse explains itself. The rafters are 2 by 4's, 24 inches on centers, posts are 4 by 4's. Entry is through either lath wing. Owners are Mr. and Mrs. William M. Roth of Sausalito, Calif. The designer was John Matthias

This is not, of course, a true greenhouse at all. It is a glasshouse open at each side to a lath corridor. It would be easy enough, however, to mount glass doors between the glassed and lathed areas, and to install heat and rig up temperature and humidity controls.

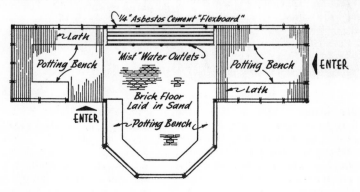

More like a glassed-in room than greenhouse. Slanting roof, louvers on top. Owners: Mr. and Mrs. H. L. Hoffman, Portland

Chrysanthemums grow to exhibition size in plastic tent on aluminum-painted iron frame. Owner: Percy A. Smith, Portland

hemisphere, and flower orchids every month in the year. You can harvest tomatoes in January and pick carnations in December. This is the world within a heated structure called a "greenhouse," a word coined hundreds of years ago to define a structure in which plants stay alive and green, while outside the same plants perish or go dormant.

However, the use of glass or its substitutes to provide shelter for plants does not necessarily imply a greenhouse. This shelter can be anything from a simple pane of glass placed over a rock plant sensitive to excess winter cold and moisture, to a coldframe housing lettuce for winter salads, to a glassed-in room off the living room or bedroom, to the latest thing in orchid houses.

Contemporary architecture and landscape architecture have added some new and exciting types of plant shelters. The use of new types of glass and plastic for covering or enclosing arbors, overhangs, lanais, porches, terraces, patios, fences, walls, and baffles now makes it possible to grow certain types of plants in sections of the garden where they could never have been grown without extra light and warmth. Naturally, these structures do not—nor are they supposed to—substitute for the greenhouse as such.

If you are an intensive gardener, you may find ways to use all or most of these different shelters. You will use a wax paper cone or cloche to cover early-started melons or tomatoes, the coldframe for your cuttings, the greenhouse for orchids, and the enclosed porch off the dining room for a collection of philodendrons or African violets.

Whatever your special interest, when the time comes for you to decide on a plant shelter, ask yourself these questions:

Do I want a purely functional shelter or one that is designed as part of the garden or house?

Do I want to use it the year around or only at special times?

Do I want to grow many different kinds of plants requiring different conditions, or only one or two kinds requiring similar conditions?

How much money can I afford to spend?

How much time can I spend taking care of my plants?

Before you make these decisions, it will be helpful to take a broad look at all the types of plant shelters available, to learn what each can do for you and approximately how much it will cost. It will also be helpful, as well as stimulating, to explore new ways in which glass and its substitutes can be used in garden design to create environments favorable both to plants and people.

On these pages we are making just such a review. We describe everything from individual plant protectors and simple coldframes on up through small pre-fab greenhouses and luxury greenhouses.

INDIVIDUAL PLANT PROTECTORS

Some individual plant covers are available ready-made; others you can easily make yourself. They are particularly useful for covering transplants or seedlings of warm weather vegetables or flowers set out ahead of the usual outdoor planting season. The farther north you live, the greater their usefulness, since they make it possible to start plants earlier and thus lengthen the normal growing season.

The paper cone, made of heavy wax paper, costs only a few cents and it will last several seasons if handled with care.

You can make the plastic wire cone (7 inches in diameter) from strips of material measuring 7 by 14 inches. These are attached to a 1-inch stick.

The plastic wire cylinder is made with a piece of material about 10 by 18 inches, shaped into a cylinder and attached to 2 pointed sticks.

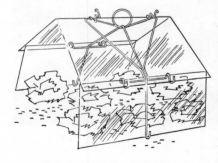

The cloche (commercially available) is a miniature wire-reenforced glass house just large enough to cover a few plants or a section of a seed row. It is made of 4 sections of glass held together with heavy galvanized wire fittings. A handle makes

Plastic sides, glass top, removable panels. Owner: Mrs. Rose White, San Rafael, Calif. Design: Katy and Paul Steinmetz

Lean-to has aluminum frame bolted to concrete base; vents at base, top. O. O. Uhle, Santa Barbara; design: Wilbur Wood

it easy to carry and also operates the ventilating system. You can remove a whole sheet of glass roof to weed or water without lifting the cloche. Sold in sets of 10 for about $30.

MULTIPLE PLANT PROTECTORS

These are portable structures which cover several plants or feet of row. To make the tunnel-like plant protector, use a piece of wire-reenforced plastic measuring 1 by 3 feet. Tack to two 3-foot strips of 1-inch wood or lath. Place the protector over the row, pressing each side into the soil to hold the protector rigid and in place.

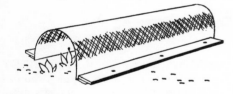

When in place, it will be about 8 inches wide and 6 inches high.

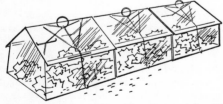

Several cloches placed end to end will make a long miniature greenhouse.

A series of frames covered with glass or plastic screen, hinged together in the center and placed tent-wise over a support, make a portable hothouse.

COLDFRAME

This under-glass garden is simple but it begins to approach the greenhouse in scope. Biggest disadvantages of the coldframe are that it doesn't accommodate the gardener along with the plants, and it can't be used to display plants. Nevertheless, with a coldframe you can do many of the same things you do in a greenhouse. Here are examples:

Early sowing—You can sow summer flowers and vegetables 8 weeks before outdoor planting time, gaining an advantage in time that often makes it possible to grow an extra crop.

Hot weather sowing—You can start vegetables, annual flowers for fall and winter color, and perennials for next year's bloom. In a coldframe they are protected from hot summer sun, and they will grow to sturdy size for setting out in fall.

Cuttings—In a coldframe you can grow cuttings of deciduous and evergreen shrubs and trees; softwood cuttings of chrysanthemums, geraniums, and fuchsias; and leaf cuttings of Rex begonias, African violets, succulents, and foliage plants. Bottom heat gives faster rooting but is not necessary, particularly in the warmer months of the year.

Winter salad greens—You can grow your own lettuce, endive, chives, parsley, and green onions right through the winter. In cold climates use bottom heat.

Forcing bulbs—Tulips, hyacinths, and daffodils, potted in early fall and kept in a cool, dark place for root development, can be placed in the frame to force early flowering for the house. Dahlia tubers can be forced in the frame to produce shoots for softwood cuttings.

Early flowers—In cold climates use the frame to bring violets, primroses, pansies, and violas into early bloom in pots.

You can make a simple and inexpensive coldframe 3 by 3 feet of 1 by 10 or 1 by 12-inch wood and cover it with a sash made of 1 by 2 or 2 by 2-inch material

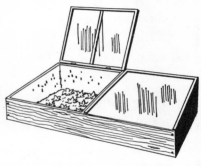

and wire-reenforced plastic. Mortise the frame or use steel angle braces at the corners, and fasten with packing case nails. Tack or staple the plastic material to the frame, then nail it down along the edges with a lath strip on all sides except the bottom. (Leave the lath strip off the bottom to permit water run-off.)

There are many kinds of coldframes on the market, of various sizes and materials. A 3 by 3½-foot model made of aluminum—which will not rust and requires no paint—sells for about $25.

For the gardener who wants an indoor

Orchids thrive in extra light provided by using only cloudy glass in upper section, clear glass below, no other shading. Radiant heating, single window with hydraulic controls. Air conditioning by Wilbur Wood, designer

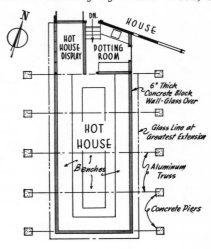

Aluminum-trussed greenhouse adjoins residence of Miss Esther Hay and Mrs. Florence Hart, Arcadia, Calif. Architects: Armet & Davis

propagating and growing case, there is the lightweight portable greenhouse which can be placed on a stand, table, or sawhorses at bench height. A commercial model comes equipped with a thermostatically controlled heating unit.

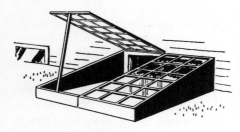

If, as in many homes in colder climates, your furnace is under the house, you can heat the frame by placing it against a basement window.

SASH GREENHOUSES

You can build a greenhouse with a standard 3 by 6-foot hotbed or coldframe sash, supported on a low wooden frame. Commercial growers in some areas use them for starting early vegetables and annuals.

Disadvantages of this type of greenhouse are that it does not admit as much light as regular sash bar greenhouses and so may be difficult to ventilate.

The simplest type of sash greenhouse is the lean-to built against the south side of a garage or fence. The sashes are supported on a low wall framed with 2 by 4 or 2 by 6-inch members. If more than one row of sashes is used, the upper row should overlap the lower one to make a water-tight roof. However, a home gardener is not likely to need a greenhouse over 6 feet wide—or the length of a hotbed sash.

The 1-sided or uneven-span sash greenhouse is well adapted to a sidehill location. Sometimes a single row of sashes is used on the uphill side and 2 or more rows on the downhill side.

Because all sash greenhouses are built with low sidewalls, you have to excavate the walk to get sufficient headroom. This is practical only where drainage is good and the soil is not too difficult to dig. Where drainage is poor, or soil is stony, it is more practical to build higher side-

walls than to excavate the path. Higher sidewalls also appeal to anyone who objects to carrying loads up and down steps. Advantages of low sidewalls are reduced initial costs and—particularly in colder climates—lower heating costs.

THE GREENHOUSE

Almost every serious gardener reaches a point where he wants a greenhouse. Whether he needs it as well is something he should consider carefully before he buys or builds one. Large numbers of greenhouses stand empty, are poorly managed, or are used for storage of everything but plants because they weren't really needed, gardeners didn't know how to use them, or they never found time to keep them up.

This is a safe rule of thumb when you begin to shop around for a greenhouse: don't get too large a one. It's easier to find room for just one more plant in a small greenhouse than it is to find time to tend a greenhouse that is too large.

Let your skill and interest dictate the size of your greenhouse. It's easy to add

often find ways to combine his gardening and his living

CHAS. R. PEARSON

Lean-to greenhouse attached to end of house extends long roofline, is enjoyed as all-year indoor garden by its owners, Mr. and Mrs. Alan Rogers, Ellensburg, Washington. Architect: Paul Thiry, Seattle

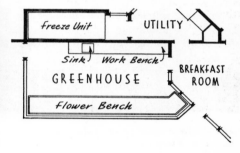

Left, enter greenhouse through breakfast room. Right, greenhouse interior. Bench at left has bottom heat; potting bench and sink at right. Fluorescent lights overhead

a section—particularly if you get one of the knockdown sectional types—when your orchid collection or propagating experiments have expanded to the point where your small greenhouse can't take another pot or square foot of cutting bed.

No matter how small your greenhouse, it should include certain standard features.

Framework. The framework should be sturdy and resistant to rot and corrosion. The material can be select redwood heart, clear, dry cedar, steel, or aluminum. Aluminum costs approximately $17\frac{1}{2}$ per cent more than steel.

In general, greenhouse experts prefer a metal framework because metal sections are narrower and cast less shadow. Home gardeners, on the other hand, frequently prefer natural wood as a pleasanter-looking material for use in a garden setting.

Glass or glass substitutes. Usually glass is favored over the glass fiber-reenforced plastics. It is cheaper and it lets in more light.

On the other hand, some manufacturers now furnish special greenhouses with plastic roofs. If properly pigmented, plastics will filter out most of the detrimental ultraviolet rays. If the plastic is reenforced with glass fiber, it will withstand most hailstorms and rocks children might throw. A light yellow colored plastic provides the highest light transmission and still filters out the harmful ultraviolet rays. Glass fiber diffuses more light than glass.

Disadvantages of plastic are its cost, its tendency to become brittle and shatter easily during extreme cold, and its greater tendency to cause condensation.

A sandblasted glass now available will absorb considerably more light than plain glass. Due to the prismatic effects of sandblasting, diffusion is equal or superior to that of glass substitutes.

Pitch. Adequate roof pitch is very important. Too slight a pitch causes drip from moisture which condenses on the under surfaces of the glass and drops on the plants below. A quarter-pitch—or a rise one-quarter of the span—seems to be a standard pitch used by many greenhouse manufacturers. All roof glazing bars should have drip grooves milled in the sides.

Foundation. Your greenhouse should stand on some kind of footing or foundation. In cold winter climates, or anywhere in heavy soils that tend to expand when wet and contract when dry, it is advisable to have a poured concrete footing. For small greenhouses in mild-climate sections, foundations of redwood (heart grade) properly treated with a wood preservative will last for many years. You can also use one course of concrete blocks (4 by 6 by 12 inches) laid without mortar. Such a foundation has the advantage of a constant but very small amount of ventilation between the uncemented blocks.

Floor. The best type of greenhouse floor is level ground covered with 2 inches of $\frac{1}{2}$-inch gravel. This is one case where the cheapest material is best. A gravel floor will stay clean, is never muddy, allows drip from watering plants to disappear into the ground, and, when kept wet on hot, dry summer days, gives off moisture to humidify the air.

Outside finishing. Any outside paint of good quality is satisfactory for the exterior woodwork. For a white exterior an

Wall forms 2 sides, supports glass top, upper walls of greenhouse off patio. Wilbur Wood, designer

WORK   STORAGE   GROWING

Work center combines 7 by 9-foot greenhouse, potting, storage area. Owners: Mr. and Mrs. Raymond Hornby, Jr., Kentfield, Calif. Design: Larry Halprin

'LTZ" paint, containing lead, titanium, and zinc, is good. Although some gardeners object to its shiny appearance, aluminum paint will last longer than regular paint. New aluminum paints now being developed offer the advantage of color.

Putty. It is a good idea to bed the glass in a permanently elastic glazing or calking compound of the best quality. Some manufacturers use a plastic putty which stays soft against the glass and forms a light crust on the outside. It does not

have to be replaced.

The old-style linseed oil and whiting in putty will hold up almost indefinitely if the exposed surfaces of the putty are painted every 3 or 4 years.

Heating. You will need to heat your green-

If you buy a stock greenhouse your choice is wide . . .

You can buy prefabricated knockdown greenhouses framed in wood, aluminum, or steel in sizes ranging from a 6 by 3-foot minimum to commercial models 18 feet wide by 150 feet long, with prices ranging

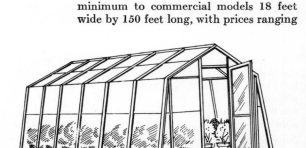

Full length aluminum . . .
Aluminum frame, full length glass on sides. Size: about 9½ by 13 feet. The sills fasten to a shallow concrete footing

Wood frame, wood base . . .
Minimum size 8 feet 9 inches by 11 feet 5 inches. Ventilators under the benches. A similar model has vents above the benches instead of below

Wood frame, expandable . . .
Size: 7x9 feet. Hinged roof sashes at top for ventilation control. Can be enlarged by adding 3-foot sections

Gardenias, fuchsias, and a lemon tree winter safely in lean-to made of window sections. Owner: Silas Gaiser, Salem, Oregon

Entrance to this greenhouse is through living room door. Concrete foundation; heat supplied through windows of basement

house if you intend to grow orchids, anthuriums, tropical ferns, or other tender plants. Heat is practically imperative if you live in a cold climate and want to use the greenhouse the year around.

Warm air systems, either with or without circulating fans, are used very successfully even in large commercial greenhouses. The cost of the operation varies with the local cost of fuels. Electric heat is expensive, except in areas where a very low power rate is available. Where natural gas is available, gas heat will cost about one-fourth as much as electric heat. A warm air system with automatic controls, using natural gas fuel, will cost about $120 to install for a greenhouse 9 by 15 feet in size.

accordingly. Below are six typical garden-size models. All of these basic types are available from manufacturers, although the sizes and designs may vary somewhat from year to year. Prices (not counting benches, heater, and other extras) range from about $225 to $600 for those shown. To equip a 7 by 9-foot wooden frame greenhouse with benches, heater, and automatic ventilator and humidity controls would cost between $125 and $150. For complete information on stock greenhouses available in your area, see the yellow pages of your telephone directory, under the listing "Greenhouse Builders."

Aluminum on masonry . . .
Aluminum - and - glass structure on masonry walls. Lengths are standardized by manufacturers

Half greenhouse, metal frame . . .
Many free-standing greenhouse models are also available in a lean-to version. This is a variation of model at left, below

Metal frame, curved eaves . . .
Steel or aluminum frame, curved eave. This version has rows of flat glass panels, angled to form a "curve." In some models, the glass itself is curved

GREENHOUSES 37

1.

... to create a garden work center

To make a small stock greenhouse fit smoothly into an over-all garden design, the landscape architect designed this generous superstructure of redwood lath.

Not only does the lath shelter help modify the conventional lines of the greenhouse, but it also provides a fortunate proportion of shade and sun in the greenhouse and lathhouse workshop. Shade plants thrive in the lathhouse, and the greenhouse glass doesn't have to be painted in the summer to reduce heat and glare. In areas where full winter sun is wise, sections of lath over the greenhouse might be removable.

The landscape architect was Douglas Baylis. Owner: Paul Byrne of San Carlos, California.

Storage space *is plentiful below the waist-high potting bench that runs along the inside walls of the lathhouse. Compacted redrock was used for the "floor"*

How to use the small stock greenhouse

2.

... to build a garden studio or den

If you enjoy working in a studio, study, or workshop in the garden—rather than in the house—you might consider making unorthodox use of an inexpensive prefabricated greenhouse.

The canvas shade projected over the greenhouse shown at right makes it an all-year studio in central California, but it could also be used for a shorter season in areas with more extreme climate.

On warm days, the shade reduces overhead heat and light. On cool days, with the shade rolled up, the studio gathers heat from the sun, needs only an occasional boost from a small space heater.

Garden greenhouse studio *for commercial artist has an adjustable canvas shade. The owner can push back canvas to let in winter sun or screen out summer sun and heat before it gets inside the structure. Friction of bamboo poles against wood frame holds*

View from the house. *"Remodeled" garden work center has cover of redwood lath*

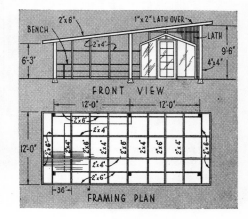

Greenhouse *is standard prefabricated variety, painted to match stain on redwood. Shade makes work area inside greenhouse comfortable even on a warm day*

in (1) work center (2) garden studio

canvas in place. The owner is James Cutter of Los Altos, California. Landscape architects: Osmundson & Staley

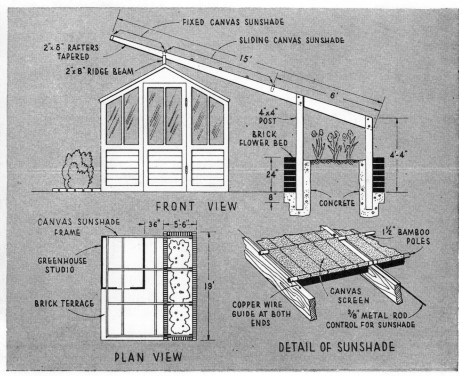

More glass-and-lath combinations . . .

Display area for pot gardener . . .

Although primarily for display, this could become a work center by placing a potting bench behind pot shelves. If lath structure faces south or west, the greenhouse will receive maximum amount of sunlight

Plant display and work center . . . with coldframes

Work and plant display center for a corner of terrace or patio. Elevated frame becomes a convenient, bench-height greenhouse and showcase for potted plants. Pulleys with counterweights make it easy to raise sash. With heat, frame can be used for orchids and other tropical plants. If you wanted to use it for cuttings, starting seedlings, bottom heat would be sufficient

The garden center in plain view . . .

Small greenhouse is the focal point in this 16 by 18-foot lathed-over area. An ideal arrangement for a section of the garden that is seen from the house or terrace, since it is primarily a growing and display center, not a work or storage area

This **south-facing** *lean-to greenhouse is 8 feet by 20 feet. Situated between sidewalk and basement-level bedroom, it becomes colorful conservatory in the winter months*

Pliable *¼-inch rubber hose handy for selective watering in greenhouse. Attached to water pipe with reducer, brass petcock*

Greenhouse over a window well

A basement window well suggested the location of this lean-to greenhouse built by Dr. Todd Gilmore of Portland. Since the bottom of the well was just below the bottom of the windows, further excavation was necessary. Aluminum, bought in 20-foot lengths and then cut to proper size, forms the overhead framework.

In summer, when the outdoor gardens are a riot of color, the greenhouse is used only as a place to start seed and hold over plants. In the fall and winter, it becomes the display place for plants.

A drain tile, leading down from the downspout and then across the property, prevented excavation at one end of the

Three bins, *25 by 23 inches, hold potting materials. A 38 by 23-inch potting bench is part of the greenhouse work center*

greenhouse (see photograph of interior). A retaining wall, built up beneath the pipe, converted this corner into a ground bed, ideal for permanent, deep rooted plants. Strelitzia, bougainvillea, gardenias, pleroma, and hoya grow in this area.

In winter the greenhouse is heated with a 220-volt portable electric fan-heater. It is thermostatically controlled for an average night temperature of 55°. Bamboo roll-down blinds are used to shade the glass on hot, sunny days.

Half the greenhouse is equipped with surface water lines fitted with half circle type sprinkler heads for surface irrigation. Rubber tubing is attached to water lines on the other side for selective watering. In a small greenhouse, this light rubber tubing is preferable to an ordinary hose, which would be too heavy and bulky. Under the eave bar, another water line, fitted with fog nozzles, provides humidity on hot, dry days.

Carnations *are planted in raised beds. Cyclamen in pots are plunged in vermiculite. Ferns grow under benches. Ground bed on the far side is used for permanent planting*

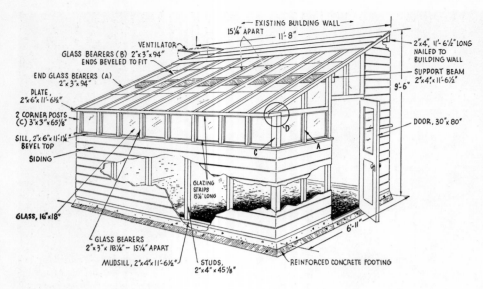

EXISTING BUILDING WALL
15¼" APART
11'-8"
VENTILATOR
GLASS BEARERS (B) 2"x3"x94"
ENDS BEVELED TO FIT
END GLASS BEARERS (A)
2"x3"x94"
PLATE,
2"x6"x11'-6½"
2 CORNER POSTS
(C) 3"x3"x65⅝"
SILL, 2"x6"x11'-1¼"
BEVEL TOP
SIDING
GLASS, 16"x18"
GLASS BEARERS
2"x3"x18¼"–15¼" APART
MUDSILL, 2"x4"x11'-6½"
STUDS,
2"x4"x45⅛"
GLAZING
STRIPS
15¼" LONG
REINFORCED CONCRETE FOOTING
2"x4", 11'-6½" LONG
NAILED TO
BUILDING WALL
SUPPORT BEAM
2"x4"x11'-6½"
9'-6"
DOOR, 30"x80"
6'-11"

How to build a
simple lean-to greenhouse

Plans for owner-built greenhouses are as flexible as a gardener's habits. Any gardener can vary the exact size of his particular greenhouse to fit his own ambitions and available garden space.

Here is a simple lean-to greenhouse built by Don Round of South Colby, Washington. If you are handy with tools and have a little time, you should be able to build a similar greenhouse for about $100.

HAVE A SOUND FOOTING
Footing should be solid, with a level, flat surface at least 4 inches wide. It might be bricks or stones mortared together. You might even soak the mudsill of 2 by 4's, 2 by 6's or 4 by 4's with rot preventive and lay it directly on the ground.

A concrete footing, however, is best. You will need about half a cubic yard, mixed one part cement, two parts sand, three parts aggregate. Reinforce with iron rod, pipe, or scrap. A concrete footing should

be about 8 inches deep, 4 inches wide on top, and taper out to 6 inches wide at the bottom.

FRAMING LUMBER MUST BE STRAIGHT
If the lumber in a greenhouse frame isn't dry and straight, the whole building will gradually sag. Either redwood or cedar makes good greenhouse framing. Ideally, wood should be painted or soaked in pentachlorophenol or copper solution before assembly. This will help prevent mold bacteria and termites. Don't use creosote on any surface which you intend to paint.

The 2 by 4-inch support beam holds the glass bearers evenly spaced, and helps prevent gradual sag. Do not hang anything from this beam, unless you support it with a post.

Nail on siding and you are ready to glaze. Whatever siding you pick will depend upon what is compatible with your house or other garden structures.

GLASS BY THE BOX
Glass comes in boxes of 50 square feet, which is cheaper than buying it in single

sheets. Each 16 by 18-inch pane contains two square feet, so there are 25 panes to a box. Get single strength "B" glass.

INSTALLING GLASS
Glass bearers are notched as indicated in the sketch, so that water condensing on the underside of the glass can run down, instead of dripping from the ceiling. You can cut these grooves easily with a small table saw. Sand them so water can't be sidetracked by a sliver.

Either glazing nails or ¾-inch galvanized tacks will hold the lower edge of the glass. Lap the sheets, 2 inches on the roof, an inch on vertical sides. Install the glass from a scaffold inside. When you have to repair a break, remove it the same way. It isn't necessary to putty.

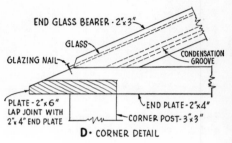

END GLASS BEARER · 2"x 3"
GLASS
GLAZING NAIL
CONDENSATION GROOVE
PLATE - 2"x 6"
LAP JOINT WITH
2"x 4" END PLATE
END PLATE - 2"x 4"
CORNER POST - 3"x 3"
D · CORNER DETAIL

VENTILATION
Fresh air circulates through the door and the hinged ventilator. Best spot for the ventilator is at the top, at the end opposite the door. Entry of air can be controlled by a notched stick propping up the cover. If insects are a problem in your garden, use screens wherever there is an opening. The door might have a small window which can be opened and closed.

A second-hand door which can take the weather will do, but get your door first. Then adjust the door opening in your plans to fit it.

GET MAXIMUM BENCH SPACE
The usefulness of any greenhouse can be measured by the square feet of bench space. Install the bench at a convenient height, and don't be afraid to make it as deep as possible. It's better to have to reach a little to get at flats or pots in the corners, than to cut down on your bench space and make it too narrow.

The sketch of the interior shows one workable arrangement. Growing space is 30 inches, wide enough to accommodate two flats side by side. The alley is wide enough for work at the bench, but you might have to turn sidewise to bend down. Extra flats, pots, and potting mixtures are stacked under the bench. Leave spaces between the boards of the bench top to allow for drainage. And don't store anything under the bench which can't take water.

You can alter the size or shape of this greenhouse to suit your garden and gardening habits, but don't make too many changes until you've figured out how your bench layout will go.

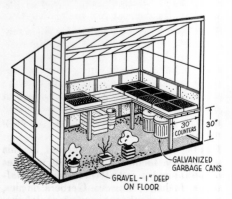

30" COUNTERS
30"
GALVANIZED
GARBAGE CANS
GRAVEL - 1" DEEP
ON FLOOR

Bench top holds flats two deep. Under bench for storage of flats and potting soil

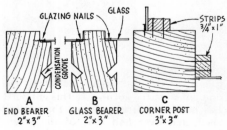

GLAZING NAILS   GLASS
CONDENSATION GROOVE
STRIPS ¾"x1"
A
END BEARER
2"x3"
B
GLASS BEARER
2"x3"
C
CORNER POST
3"x3"

Cross-section views. Angular cuts in glass bearers act as gutters for condensation

Owner-built garden structure designed for a Northwest garden. Greenhouse is on the left. Potting shed on right. Glass covered — *entry flanked by decorative Chinese tiles. Brick plant box on either side of the entry helps tie the building into garden site*

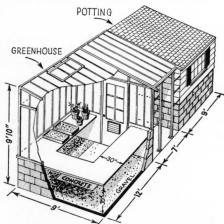

Floor is a concrete slab except under the greenhouse benches, which is sand, kept wet in order to maintain high humidity

Nearing completion, greenhouse is still without brick plant box or Chinese tiles

Greenhouse and potting shed are connected by an entry-passageway

Many gardeners think only in terms of climate control when they build greenhouses.

However, this greenhouse, designed and built by the owner, Richard W. Faville of Portland, goes far beyond that. It not only supplies growing and work space, it also contributes to the landscape design.

Although all in one building, greenhouse functions are sharply divided by the floor plan. Face the entry, and space on the left is for growing and display. On the right is the potting shed for storage of soil mixtures, tools, pots. Here dirty work can be carried on without taking valuable growing space away from the greenhouse itself.

The wide, glassed-over entry is as inviting as the entrance hall of a house. It offers a protected area for plant boxes of begonias, pots of fuchsias, and also makes a covered passageway between greenhouse and potting shed.

Some gardeners might question the amount of space devoted to this entry. It has nearly as much area as the potting shed, and over half that of the greenhouse. It is the generous entry, however, which makes this greenhouse interesting.

AUTOMATIC WEATHER INSIDE

Climate controls for the greenhouse are all automatic, with the exception of humidification. Two thermostatically controlled electric heaters, equipped with fans, are under the benches. Bottom heat for propagating comes from a heating cable laid down in the bench soil. This, too, is thermostatically controlled.

All direct drafts on plants have been eliminated by using blowers which can change a thousand cubic feet of air a minute, inhaling it through louvers under the door, exhaling it through an opening in the upper part of the side wall. There are no roof ventilators.

Condensation which runs down the underside of the glass roof can drip through a three-inch gap left between benches and walls, into a bed of sand and soil which is kept wet under the benches to help maintain high humidity.

Plants which have been grown in this greenhouse include: orchids, 30 varieties of geraniums, a jade tree, hyacinths, daffodils, fuchsias, hibiscus, Gerbera daisies, begonias, magnolias, a wax plant, lobelia, phlox, pansies, violas.

Greenhouse utilizes self-bracing construction of the A-frame. Redwood was used throughout. Sheets of plastic held in place by battens. Lightweight reed screen covers the east side to help shade it from morning sun. Nearby garage shades west side

Plastic A-frame . . . quick and inexpensive

When the Charles Kasslers of Glendora, California, needed quick cover for their newly acquired collection of cattleya orchids, they decided to adapt the A-frame idea to their greenhouse needs. The result was this simple, self-bracing structure, covered with polyethylene. Total cost of materials was approximately $75 (1959). It was built in just two days.

1"X 2" DIAGONAL BRACE

CLEAR PLASTIC LOUVER 18"X 46"

1"X 12" REDWOOD

1"X 3" REDWOOD CROSS BRACE

10' 6"

2"X 4" REDWOOD FRAME 16" CENTERS

3'

2"X 6" REDWOOD

1"X 2"

REDWOOD BENCH 1"X 2" SLATS 2" APART

PEA GRAVEL FLOOR

14'

15'

Simplicity of A-frame makes it easy for the do-it-yourself'er. Sunset book, Cabins and Vacation Houses, has A-frame ideas

Interior view. Slat bench at left holds pots of orchids; used also for flats. Pea gravel keeps earth floor from getting muddy

Inexpensive *kerosene heater can be called into service on cold winter nights*

The plan used here could be modified quite easily to fit many situations. Wood members in this structure are redwood, ideally suited to greenhouse use. In some areas, cedar could be used with equal effectiveness.

Precut sides and bench material to simplify handling. You can arrange to have a lumber yard do this for you. Add a wood preservative to the 2-inch by 6-inch redwood base where wood touches the ground. Use galvanized nails and hinges throughout the structure.

There is no lost space inside. Under the bench there's room for cuttings and seeds in flats, and a place for small potted plants. On the cross braces are hooks for hanging baskets.

Last winter a simple kerosene heater was used when necessary. The pea gravel used as floor material provides fast drainage, and is easy to walk on.

In addition to the cattleya orchids, the Kasslers also grow cymbidiums, fuchsias, ferns, hibiscus, gardenias, *Hoya carnosa*, camellia cuttings, tomato seedlings, ferns, macadamia seedlings, petunia seedlings, and elephant ear sprouts in their greenhouse.

List of Materials
(Cedar or Redwood)

1	piece	1″ x 12″ x 15′
20	pieces	2″ x 4″ x 12′
2	—	2″ x 6″ x 14′
20	—	1″ x 2″ x 12′
6	—	2″ x 4″ x 8′
1	—	1″ x 12″ x 15′
3	—	1″ x 2″ x 18′
2	—	2″ x 6″ x 15′
30	—	1″ x 2″ x 30″
3	—	1″ x 2″ x 15′

580 square feet of polyethylene

Greenhouse-work center as seen from bedroom area of house. Redwood grapestake walls blend into a background of trees. White-painted glass in the greenhouse section

Greenhouse and workroom in one

Greenhouse and workroom were combined in a structure of redwood and white-painted glass which blends easily into its garden setting. Standard greenhouse construction might have been slightly less expensive, but far less in harmony with the surroundings.

The glass-roofed greenhouse portion is heated by a coil of the radiant heat system running out from the house. The coil is then brought up from the concrete slab to heat a shelf for tropical plants.

The unheated workroom has a sink and counter for potting, and storage space for garden equipment.

Architects: Confer and Ostwald. Owners: Mr. and Mrs. Archie Andrews, Piedmont, California.

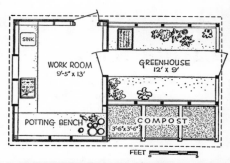

Interior of workshop, with a galvanized metal counter for dirty work, bins for dry storage, and drawers to hold working tools

Built-in compost bins behind greenhouse (opposite side from view above). Retaining wall hides incinerator from the house

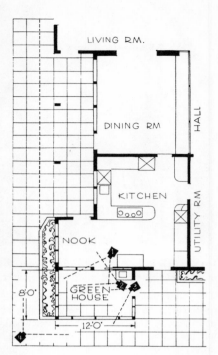

Plan *shows greenhouse's relation to rooms. Numbers key camera angles to photos*

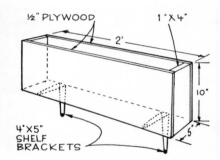

Sketch *of simple garden tool holder shown upper left, next page. It is merely a box filled with sand, with a little lubricating oil added to keep tools rustless, bright*

1. **Like another room,** *beyond sliding glass door and big fixed window at left, greenhouse provides a leafy, bower-like view—airy in winter, cool and shaded in the summer—that contributes to the livability of this kitchen-breakfast area. Owners can indulge their garden hobby all year—in winter without going outdoors*

This greenhouse is actually a part of the house

This greenhouse is more than just a hothouse where you can raise plants all year around. Dr. and Mrs. D. F. Bourassa of Bellevue, Washington, asked Architect Thomas Albert Smith to plan it as part of their house. It functions as a hobby room, and shows its best face to the house, giving it an indoor garden view.

You see its summer aspect pictured here —its sheltering grape vine in leaf and aluminum slats filtering the sun. In the winter, with the grape leafless and the slats down, the greenhouse seems to collect light and warmth.

This is the Bourassas' first greenhouse, and they are having fun with it. Neither has developed a specialty yet, but Dr. Bourassa likes to propagate plants and experiment with cuttings. He designed and built the tool holder and slat sun shade shown above. Mrs. Bourassa has had good luck with hibiscus cuttings— her plants are blooming on a nearly year-around schedule—and with tuberous be-

gonias, geranium cuttings, African violets, and foliage plants for interior decoration. The greenhouse is a glass covered lean-to type, available commercially. It is heated by radiant coils from the central heating system of the house, set in the concrete floor. A temperature of 60° to 65° is maintained, bolstered during periods of extreme cold by an electric heater. The Bourassas chose the 10 by 16-foot size. It allows them room enough to work in the greenhouse together.

2. **Inside greenhouse,** *looking toward breakfast area. Note sink and counter. One of two ventilating fans is at upper left*

3. **Bench at left** *has electric bottom heat. Aluminum slats let in some light but reflect heat, are taken down in winter*

ELIZABETH GREEN

4. **Greenhouse separates** *outdoor living area from service yard. Its outside door is near the kitchen entry (to right). Grape* *vine, planted for shade on south side, produces abundant crop because of warmth, keeps out summer heat, lets in winter light*

Remodeled to include a glassed-in garden

The owners of this Portland home don't have to walk out into the garden to enjoy their greenhouse activities.

When the house was remodeled, the greenhouse was planned as a part of the ground floor addition. Also on this ground floor is a recreation room and small bathroom, a workshop, and a large storage closet.

The glass wall of the greenhouse faces southwest, taking advantage of sunshine the year around. In any climate where heat from the sun might pose a problem, you could install a roll bamboo blind outside the glass for summertime use.

Owners: Mr. and Mrs. David Robinson. The architect was Walter Gordon.

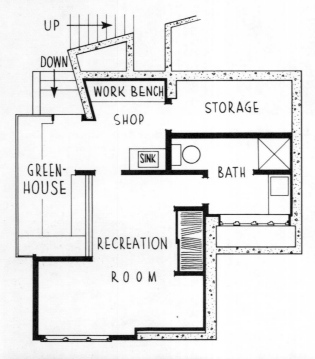

Greenhouse *is built on ground level of addition to the original house shown in the background. Deck over the greenhouse is directly off large living room-bedroom, which has a separate outside entrance*

Central heating *system supplies heat and is controlled by sliding sheet metal dampers. Greenhouse framework is aluminum*

Glass partition *separates greenhouse from the recreation room. Bamboo blinds on traverse rods can be drawn to block sun glare*

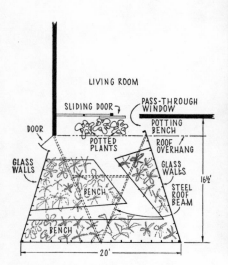

Plan *shows how greenhouse walls angle from house to an end wall 20 feet wide*

Greenhouse addition, *extending from the living room wall of this house, was built on spot formerly occupied by patio. Note clear, unpainted glass on the north wall*

Greenhouse alongside the living room

Because the greenhouse is located on the north side of the house, it loses about 5 feet of growing space for plants that specifically need sun. Although most indoor plants will grow perfectly in this zone, Mr. Rees finds that some orchids and bromeliads fail to bloom if raised in this shaded area.

WILLIAM APLIN

A greenhouse directly off the living room is one of the most attractive features in the home of Mr. and Mrs. Benjamin Rees of Pasadena.

Quite early in their planning, it was clear that the logical spot to add a greenhouse was the concrete-paved patio just north of the living room. The floor was in, and there was already a 10-foot-square wall of glass with sliding doors between living room and patio area.

In the course of sketching out ideas for the greenhouse addition, Mr. Rees hit on the splayed floor plan and the folded roof that terminates in a gable end wall.

The splayed shape gets more floor space under glass without overlapping another 10 feet of living room wall. The high-centered, folded roof creates a more-interesting-than-usual pattern when viewed from inside the house (see the photograph at right) and allows the entire roof structure to be supported on only one post, centered in the gable end wall. The structural frame is aluminum. The glass is painted white on both the east and west walls and the roof. The floor area beyond the original concrete patio is covered with gravel, to provide drainage.

The Reeses keep the doors to the living room closed to maintain the proper temperature and humidity. Temperatures are controlled automatically—a cooler switches on at 83°, a heater at 60°. Humidity is controlled by "feel," with the evaporative cooler providing sufficient humidity most of the time.

The heater, devised by Mr. Rees, consists of a 20-gallon hot water heater and a fan to circulate the air over copper coils that carry the hot water. Mr. Rees says this heating system has proved a convenient solution to another of his greenhouse chores. He prefers to water plants with warm water, so the 20-gallon tank provides an immediate and abundant supply.

View from living room. *Benches are angled for continuous display. Only plants in show condition are kept on forward benches. Aluminum framed benches with pipe supports have airy quality*

With doors open wide, the display of rhododendrons, Rex begonias, camellias, and other plants can be enjoyed from living room

To live with plants the year around . . .

This Northwest greenhouse succeeds in doing a rare thing. Outside, it blends with the garden. Inside, it becomes part of the house. It extends the living room with an indoor garden where seasonal and warm weather plants can put on an all-year daily show. Designed by the owner, Mr. Endre Ostbo, Bellevue, Washington.

Greenhouse room is 12 by 16 feet. Glass is held between 2 by 2-inch upright supports. Note how roof follows house roof-line

Concrete slab floor with dirt planting beds around the edges of room. The door at right leads directly outside to the garden

A greenhouse can be a part of the family room . . .

Glass addition is used for early seed sowing and overwintering of tender plants. Owners: Mr. and Mrs. John Weaver, Seattle

Greenhouse extension brings color into Weavers' family room. This way it can be enjoyed many more hours than if detached

. . . or it can be related to the outdoor living room

CHARLES R. PEARSON

This structure gains in lightness through the use of narrow steel bars. Roof and lower section of door are of blue corrugated plastic. Cost of plastic is greater than glass but work of installa- *tion is easier. Including the greenhouse directly in the outdoor living area as done here has both social and practical advantages. Owners are Mr. and Mrs. Lyman W. Thomas, Seattle*

"Greenhouses in miniature"

For many gardeners, it is not practical to take on the responsibilities of a real, full-sized greenhouse. But for those who like to grow things in small or medium quantity, there is the greenhouse's baby brother—the coldframe.

A coldframe gives you a jump on spring. When winter is doing its worst, a coldframe's few cubic feet of warmth and shelter can be giving birth to a large portion of next year's garden. Cuttings are taking root, seeds are germinating, seedlings are growing on to a size where they can be set out in the garden to make it on their own.

When it comes to growing annuals, a coldframe gives you more than a jump on spring. Seeds sown in a frame will bloom several weeks earlier than seed sown in open ground. When cool days and clammy soil discourage seed germination in open ground, a coldframe allows you to manufacture and control a capsule of weather. You can provide for near maximum seed germination conditions. By the time the weather is right, you have sturdy little plants to set in your garden.

You'll get the best use from your coldframe if it is convenient to the house, near a hose connection, and set out of the wind. Expert gardeners agree that frames facing south or southeast give best results because they gain the maximum advantage of spring sunshine. Sun can quickly build up 100° heat in a closed frame, so you'll need to pay especial attention to ventilating, watering, and shading in this exposure, but you can grow good thrifty plants.

A frame in filtered sun beneath trees gets tempered sunshine. Although a frame in this location won't need such careful supervision as if it were completely exposed, artificial shading, watering, and ventilating are still necessary. Plants grow leggy if they must reach for light.

STANDARD COLDFRAMES

Millwork plants and most lumber companies carry standard coldframe sash in 3 by 4 or 3 by 6-foot sections, or you can use discarded window or French door sash. Regular coldframe sash, filled in with small overlapping panes of glass called "lights," allows both rain and condensed moisture inside the frame to drain off. Large single panes of glass work just as well—in fact, they admit more light—but the breakage and replacement factors are a problem.

Glass is still a standard choice for roofing a coldframe. Small panes are inexpensive, easy to replace, and let in a maximum of light. Plastic impregnated wire lets in nearly as much light and costs less, but it deteriorates with age and tends to grow cloudy. Flexible sheet plastics, such as polyethylene, while tough, are not permanent. Corrugated or flat structural plastic lasts longer than glass, but costs more.

Usually, a transparent roof hinges to the coldframe box that has been set an inch or more into the ground. The sides of the box, made of 2 by 12's, are cut at an angle so the roof slopes, to let in a maximum of light as well as drain off moisture. A standard frame measures approximately 10 to 12 inches high at the back, 6 to 8 inches at the front.

It's worthwhile to protect lumber used in a permanent coldframe with one of the paint-on preservatives containing copper napthenate or pentachloralphenol. Don't use creosote—it releases fumes in hot weather that may damage plants. Some lumber yards sell lumber treated with a pressurized salt preservative; this doesn't change the wood or endanger plants. You can take pre-cut lumber to a preservative plant for pressure salt treating. The cost is about 70 cents per 18 board feet of lumber.

An efficient coldframe is as airtight as

"Four-door" model lets you work in a section at a time. Plastic sifts out strong sunlight. Upright supports the sash when open

possible. Seal cracks with batten, line the frame with building paper, and use weather stripping to make the top snug. Soil or sawdust banked against the outside helps insulate against cutting winds.

HOW TO USE A COLDFRAME

All coldframes, permanent or makeshift, work on the same principles. If you understand them, you'll be able to manage yours to its best advantage. Here are some suggestions for controlling moisture, temperature, and light in a coldframe:

Shade it from the direct sun. This can be done by covering the glass with light muslin, whitewash, or, in an emergency, muddy water. One gardener attaches a light, roller-type window blind to his frame, and he pulls it down as needed.

When watering plants inside the coldframe, use a fine spray and tepid water to avoid dislodging or shocking seedlings.

Ventilate the coldframe by raising the sash on warm days.

Cover the coldframe with a blanket at night if a temperature below 40° has been predicted.

Keep the coldframe clean by removing dead leaves and plants.

A coldframe can provide shelter for pests as well as plants. Spray the interior with a good insecticide and set out slug bait continuously.

Inside a coldframe, you can plant directly into prepared soil or in movable flats or pots. In the latter case, put a 3 or 4-inch layer of sand, sharp gravel, or cinders in your coldframe for quick drainage.

ART HUPY

Glass door sash *set at a steep pitch, with a convenient handle added, makes an excellent, tight cover for a coldframe*

If mullions *of the door or window sash are notched, the water drains off quickly. Design: Harry Davidson, Bellevue, Wash.*

How to build a heated coldframe

Controllable heat can widen a coldframe's range of usefulness. In this example—developed by the Agricultural Engineering Department of the Puget Sound Power & Light Company—the heat comes from light bulbs mounted on the sash supports.

The three center supports may be lifted free from the frame to allow more working space. The sash can be lifted from the supports, or it can be slid up or down on the waxed surfaces.

Face the frame due south; set into the ground 12 inches and bank high outside with dirt. Use dressed cedar lumber (or redwood), treated with a preservative. Bulb sockets should be weather-proof; all wire splices soldered, then wrapped with rubber tape and friction tape. Wedge outlets at a slant so that moisture will drain free. Use 10- or 15-ampere fuses; disconnect main switch before working in frame. Vary degree of heat by unscrewing desired number of bulbs, or install a thermostat.

•

Here is the list of material needed to build the frame:

Item	Size	Pcs.	Item and No.
a	2"x12"x12'4"	5	Greenhouse sash— 4 (3'x6')
b	2"x12"x6'1½"	4	Handles—4
c	2"x12"x4'9"	2	Glass, 14"x9½"—60
d	2"x 4"x8'0"	5	Wood screws
e	2"x 4"x2'7"	2	No. 14 RC wire 37 ft.
f	2"x 4"x1'7"	2	No. 12 WP wire
g	1"x 4"x3'0"	2	Split porcelain knobs
h	1"x 4"x2'6"	5	Wood preservative
i	1"x 4"x2'0"	2	Outlets—3
j	1"x 4"x1'7"	3	Cleat receptacles—12
k	1"x 1⅝"x8'0"	5	50-watt lamps—12
			Putty, paint

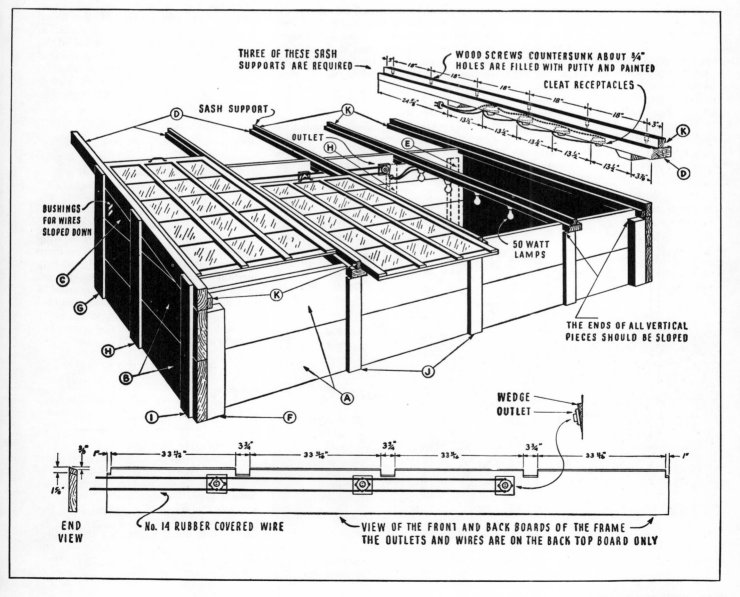

A portable case for cuttings and seedlings

Use it on the patio . . . the deck . . . even a corner of the basement

AFTER experimenting both with the most primitive of propagating arrangements—the box or pot of cuttings or seedlings on the kitchen window sill—and the more advanced type in the form of a greenhouse, we have decided that the most convenient and practical arrangement for the average gardener who wants to grow only a few plants at a time is a comparatively small, portable propagating case.

Place your propagating case on the porch, roof, or deck; the terrace, patio, sun porch, or loggia; or in a corner in the basement. Let the entire family share the fun of watching plants grow, and let them help with the upkeep, if their interest is aroused.

A small propagating unit can be built so that it operates with practically no attention. For example, in the model shown here, humidity, temperature, and light are so well controlled that the case need hardly be opened throughout the entire rooting or germination and seedling period of many faster growing species of plants.

The case illustrated here was developed by V. T. Stoutemyer and Albert W. Close at the United States Plant Introduction Garden in Glen Dale, Maryland. Although this case probably is more efficient than the average greenhouse for most propagat-ing purposes, it is easy and inexpensive to build. Since it is artificially lighted, the case can be placed without regard to sunlight. In most locations, it will be necessary to catch moisture draining from the rooting medium in a tray or through a hose or pipe.

The original model was 6 feet long, 3 feet wide, and 3 feet high. A 2-foot width might make it more practical for use in homes where the doors measure the standard 30-inch width. The case is constructed of waterproof composition board, which gives almost perfect insulation against loss of heat and prevents undue condensation of moisture.

Whatever material is used for the rest of the case, it's advisable to build the frame of metal or rot-resistant wood, such as redwood or cedar. On the front of the case are two doors hinged at the top. Although opaque doors were used in the original model, glass substitute or glass panes might be used, provided direct sunlight were not permitted to enter.

In the original model, light is provided by two 40-watt fluorescent lamps and a small reflector. Fluorescent strips, while possessing a more limited reflecting surface, can also be used. To provide maximum reflec-tion, the interior of the case should be painted white.

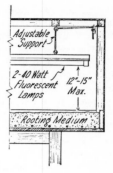

Although heating of the case may not be necessary for the successful growth of many seeds and cuttings, the installation of soil heating cables in the bottom of the case speeds rooting and germination of some species. The heating cables, installed in combination with a soil-heating thermo-stat, should be at least 4 inches under the rooting medium.

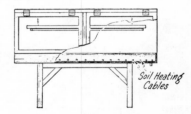

Also shown here is an alternate heating method in which a socket heater or lamp is installed in a space below the rooting medium. Available for this purpose are small sealed heating units ranging from 75 to 150 watts with bases fitting standard light sockets. Carbon filament lamps or two ordinary tungsten lamps connected in a series are other possibilities.

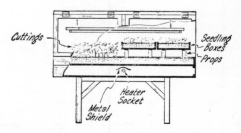

Note in the accompanying illustration that a small metal shield is placed over the socket and heating unit to prevent contact with drainage water from the rooting medium above. Placing a pan of water under the rooting medium is helpful in maintaining proper humidity.

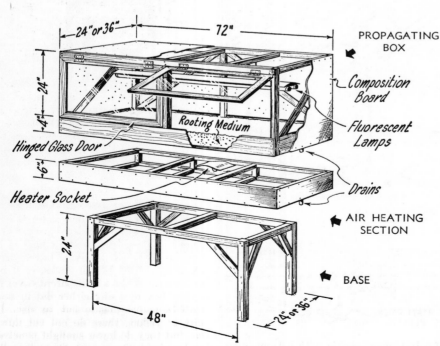

Case similar to that used in government test. Unlike original, it has glass doors to permit observation without opening case. Direct sunlight must not enter

Coldframe variations

... using glass, plastic, lath

REDUCED to its simplest form, a coldframe is a box with a transparent roof. Here are some variations for the gardener who needs a coldframe in a hurry.

If you have a plant box on the south or east side of your house, you already have the beginning of a coldframe. Rig up a transparent cover, either of glass or plastic. You may need to lower the soil level in the plant box to use it as a coldframe, but by the time you need to ready it for summer flowers, you'll be all through using it as a coldframe.

Knock out the bottom of a stout wooden box, such as an apple box. Put the bottom 2 or 3 inches into the ground. Set it at an angle to slant the pane of glass you use for a roof. The glass can be held in place

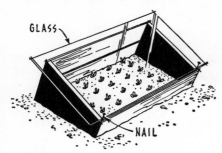

by 2 nails driven part way into the low end of the box.

The simplest protection is the European cloche idea—a small glass tent made of separate pieces of glass clipped together at the edges.

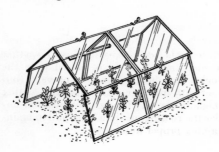

The cloche is usually built in 2-foot sections that vary in height from 9 to 24 inches and in width from 15 to 26 inches, depending on shape—tent, barn, or box. It is constructed of heavy galvanized wire and panes of double strength glass; these are clamped together in such a way that they can be taken apart easily and moved from one spot to another.

For early spring seed sowing, you can make an elevated coldframe like this.

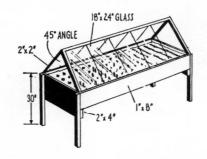

You could set up such a frame conveniently right in the garden work area. Use a lath or cheesecloth cover instead of glass in summer and you have an excellent place to sow seeds of next year's perennials.

The availability of plastics, both pliable sheets in various weights and flat or corrugated building plastic, will stimulate many ingenious adaptations of the coldframe idea. For instance, a U-frame of light lumber or 1-inch pipe thrust into the ground can become the basis for a tent

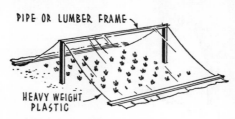

of polyethylene plastic, with bottom edges weighted with dirt, rocks, or battens.

A seed flat takes on the properties of a

coldframe if two supports are nailed on one end to hold up a piece of clear flexible

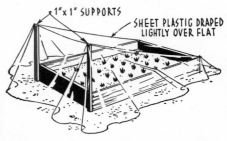

plastic. Heavy polyethylene plastic (carried by some seed stores) is meant for just this sort of use. It takes only a little more time to attach coat hangers at either end

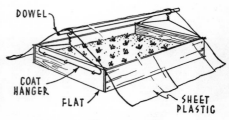

of a flat, and fasten a dowel from one hook to the other to support a sheet of flexible plastic.

If you intend to grow only a few plants, seed them in one flat and use another for a cover by knocking out the bottom of the lid flat and tacking a piece of wire-reinforced plastic over it. Place sticks at corners to lift top flat for short periods of ventilation.

One gardener we know uses an old-fashioned, large-domed skylight, picked up from a building wrecker's yard, with great success. Although it is large and too heavy to lift, its four sides, which raise up for ventilation, are big enough to work through. Some of the plastic bubble skylights can also be adapted for emergency climate control in a small area.

For a good temporary coldframe, make a rectangular box with four 1 by 6-inch boards and set it up on level ground. To strengthen its corners and to hold it in place, wedge with stakes (steel tent stakes, sharpened broom sticks, or 2 by 2's). You can make a transparent cover to fit your box by using either flat or corrugated opaque plastic cut to size. In white or yellow, these do not cut down heat, but they do lower sunlight penetration by about 30 per cent. Or make a lid by stapling wire reinforced plastic to a batten frame.

How to plan a garden work

THE GARDEN WORK CENTER
ON THE COVER

CLYDE CHILDRESS

This *photograph and the two on next page show more of work center pictured on cover. This is a potting bench. The garbage cans hold peat, compost, and sand. Racks sketched on page 59*

As a gardener how often have you wished for a place to store your tools? Wanted a dry place to keep a sack of fertilizer? Felt need of a locker for dangerous garden chemicals, a shady place for cuttings, a sturdy potting bench, a place to garden under glass? Or wanted a storage and work yard somewhere out of sight?

If any of your fond hopes are included in this list, you are in the market for some sort of garden work center. Whether you need nothing more than a well-organized place to store your tools, or want an all-out garden workshop, you should find some ideas you can use on these pages.

We've looked at a lot of garden work centers over the years, and find that many of them become catch-alls for miscellaneous storage. To prevent this, you should plan realistically.

HOW TO PLAN FOR EXPANSION

Most of the enthusiastic gardeners we know have developed their interests—and their work centers—a step at a time. Let's take a look at three typical stages in this development. The sketches show how you could start a work center with a basic storage unit and add to it as your interest grows.

Stage one—for the family with little time for gardening. If you don't do any more gardening than necessary, a storage center will make your work easier and may be all you need. Here are some features to consider; all can be handled in surprisingly small space:

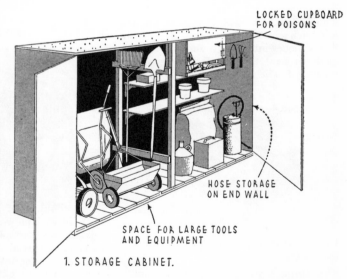

LOCKED CUPBOARD FOR POISONS

HOSE STORAGE ON END WALL

SPACE FOR LARGE TOOLS AND EQUIPMENT

1. STORAGE CABINET.

Good tool storage. Hand tools should have some protection from the weather, be easy to get at, and hung on sturdy supports.

Weatherproof shelter for rolling equipment like a mower, fertilizer spreader, and wheelbarrow. Doors should be wide and the sill low so it is easy to move the equipment in and out. If you have power equipment you also need a safe place to store oil and gasoline.

Covered enclosed cabinets for fertilizers and necessary pest and weed controls. If your materials include poisons, have a cabinet you can lock. In second-hand and war surplus stores, we've seen inexpensive wood and metal boxes that can be bolted to a wall for storing dangerous chemicals.

center . . . to fit you and your garden needs

Drawers, cupboards, or boxes for small tools like pruning shears; and for sprinklers, nozzles, hose washers.

A reel for garden hose and soakers.

Stage two—as your interest in gardening develops. If you begin to grow a few container plants, set out bulbs, annuals and perennials for seasonal color, and perhaps grow some vegetables, you can use added facilities like these:

Storage space for pots, boxes, and tubs.

A place for buckets or boxes of sand, peat, and other soil for potting mixtures.

2. WORKBENCH AND SHELVES ADDED TO BACK OF CABINET

BUCKETS AND BOXES FOR BULK STORAGE

STORAGE FOR POTS AND FLATS

A minimum work bench for potting. If you have a bench in the garage, it might double for garden work.

A protected place to overwinter a few potted plants.

A corporation yard. At this stage you may want to give space to an out-of-sight collection point for all kinds of miscellaneous storage—pipe, lumber, and other construction materials, for example.

Raised beds *provide level planting areas of good soil on a two-way slope of clay. Beds are used as a "nursery yard" for pots and small plants and for annuals and vegetables in season*

The only steps *required are at this end of the slope. Adobe set on grade paves rest of area. The large blocks are easy to lay on steps and slope, attractive with plants and the redwood*

Stage three—for the all-out garden enthusiast. As you develop special garden interests, you need specialized facilities. In this check list are features that will help an enthusiastic pot gardener or plant specialist with his work:

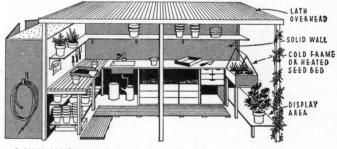

LATH OVERHEAD

SOLID WALL

COLD FRAME OR HEATED SEED BED

DISPLAY AREA

3. FINAL ADDITION MAKES A COMPLETE WORK CENTER

Large storage space for empty pots, flats, and containers.

Bins or cans for potting mix—materials like sand, peat, compost, topsoil, leaf mold, manure, pumice, charcoal.

Water supply with sink for washing pots and flats.

A sturdy work bench, planned for the kind of work you do.

Overhead protection for seedlings and small plants.

A place to garden under glass: coldframe, bottom heated cutting bench, or greenhouse.

Holding area for potted or tubbed plants not yet in bloom. Such plants usually are quite attractive at this stage. You may want to locate this area where the plants can be seen.

Storage area (out of general view) for plants that are cut back, or too small to be attractive.

WHERE SHOULD THE WORK CENTER GO?

On a city or subdivision lot, you may have to do some careful figuring to get what you want in the space you have. We have seen work centers in side yards; against a back fence; attached to a house, car port, or garage; and as part of a patio. On page 61 are sketches of work centers in small space.

No matter where you put the work center, you will probably have to make some compromises. Here are some points to keep in mind when planning the location.

It is a real advantage to have the work area close to a driveway, or have some way to drive into it. You use a lot of heavy materials in the garden—like bales of peat, yards of manure, bags of fertilizer, and brick, gravel, sand, and topsoil.

Don't forget set-back regulations and building requirements. In most towns a permit is required to build any kind of permanent structure on your property. There are also height limitations to consider.

A back corner of your lot is a good location for the work center if you need all the space up near the house for outdoor living and for lawns, flowers, trees, and shrubs. This location also helps hide the clutter that usually develops in the area.

You will want to store manure and compost piles away from the house.

If you have an incinerator you might include it in a corporation yard-work center.

On the other hand, if the work center is next to the house you will probably make a point of keeping it orderly. You may also find that you use it more.

If you are concerned about the appearance, remember that one side can be a decorative screen, plant support, or display rack. See page 61 for details on such a structure.

NARROW SIDE YARD

Sink, bench, and storage, in a space six feet wide between house and fence. Owner-builder Ben Bearse uses area to pot plants for display in rear garden of narrow San Francisco lot. Work top, back splash are of asbestos cement board. Cupboard doors are hinged at top. Landscape architect: Douglas Baylis

POTTING BENCH-COLDFRAME

This ingenious redwood and glass work center includes a bench with sheet aluminum top, three bins and two shelves for storage, and pulley operated glass top hinging down to make a coldframe. The pulleys are attached to the roof overhang above the porch. Designed and built by R. A. Windmiller, San Francisco

IN A TIGHT CORNER

High fence makes two sides of this compact work area in the James H. Parks garden in Carmel, California. Left to right: Good-sized storage cupboard with a lock, sheltered potting bench, a glass-protected corner for flats of seedlings, open planting bed, space for outside storage. Gravel underfoot

INSIDE A LATH HOUSE

Large bins for fertilizer and soil mixing materials are protected under the bench. Bins are individual units set on 2 by 2's at the base. This provides ventilation under the bins and a track to pull them out on for filling. In use, openings are large enough to reach into. There's a sink with faucet at end of bench. Neat shelves above the bench are used for storage and display of potted plants. Brick floor under bench

R. WENKAM

MOSTLY FOR DISPLAY

This attractive lath structure, for the protection and display of orchids, has a small work space at the far end—where there is room enough to work on one plant. The shelter was designed for Mr. and Mrs. William Shinner of Honolulu by Harold Whitaker. It is built against a sloping bank, and helps hold it in place. Notice that the uprights are supported on concrete piers under the bottom shelf

IDEAS FOR BULK STORAGE

Sketched below are three ideas for workshop projects that will simplify handling materials like peat, compost, and sand.

Garbage cans *are excellent containers for loose materials. On a rack like this it is easy to shovel the material out of the can*

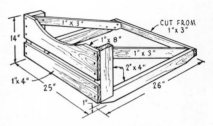

Build rack *to fit the size garbage can you have. If planned for use under a bench, tilt the can according to bench height*

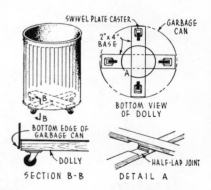

Dolly *for garbage can. Good idea if work center has concrete floor. Bottom edge of can overlaps crossbar and holds it on*

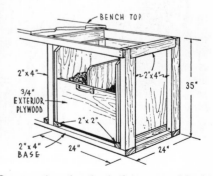

Construction detail *of the removable bin shown in the photograph at top of page. In use the bin is pulled out only when nearly empty. Sand and wax the 2x2 support and bin bottom to reduce friction*

WORK CENTERS 59

BLAIR STAPP

WILLIAM APLIN

WORK AREA OUT OF SIGHT

Completely enclosed storage yard-work center in corner of Los Angeles garden by Landscape Architect Ruth Patricia Shellhorn. Fence, back wall, and overhead lath are grapestakes. Flower pots on top of brick wall can be seen from garden on left

ART HUPY

PLASTIC ROOF ATTACHED TO GARAGE

Work center in Woodside, California, attached to side of garage. Solid area in upper left is the overhang of the garage roof. Gate at far end leads to patio. Tool storage behind bench, note faucet below. Owners: Mr. and Mrs. Richard C. Kern.

METAL BENCH TOP, STORAGE BELOW

Combination work top-storage cabinets have sheet metal top. Center section open below for bulk storage in garbage cans on casters. Storage cabinets on each end. Owners: Mr. and Mrs. J. T. Patten, Jr., Bellevue, Wash. Designer: Maury Johnson

MATERIALS YOU CAN USE

For construction. Because they are good looking, weather well, and resist decay, *redwood* and *cedar* are the most popular woods for garden construction. In the Northwest *fir* is also used; if preservative treated, it, too, resists decay and has an attractive dark color.

For overhead protection. *Lath* is used most for overhead shade in a garden work center. For straight lines with no sag, don't use anything smaller than 1x2 material. For a more rustic look, use grapestakes or split cedar lath. *Reed or bamboo screen* and *snow fencing* (lath woven in wire) are also good.

If you want a solid roof, you can use *asphalt roofing paper, plywood, hardboard,* or *asbestos board.* Or you can make a more permanent roof surfaced with asphalt or wood shingles, or with asphalt and gravel.

For a protecting roof that admits light—where it's not too hot—use *sheet plastic, plastic impregnated fiber glass,* or *glass.*

For a listing of other materials suitable for a work center (including price and description) see the *Sunset* book, *How to Build Patio Roofs.*

Work surfaces. A bench top should be reasonably weatherproof, sturdy, and easy to clean. *Spaced 2 by 2's or 2 by 3's,* about ¼ inch apart, make a strong work top that's almost self cleaning. However you can get splinters from it, and it won't hold loose materials. A solid section is a worthwhile addition.

Here are other materials we've seen used:

Exterior plywood. Paint it well, especially the edges.

Tempered hardboard. Before you install, wet it and keep under

WHERE SPACE IS NO PROBLEM

Complete garden storage center and work space at Woodside, California, home of Mr. and Mrs. L. H. Markwood. Lath overhead provides shade for plants—and gardener—most of day. Cans of soil mix on casters. Landscape architect: Gil Rovianek

MORLEY BAER

STORAGE AND WORK CENTER

Below the sink and small work counter is a shelf for small tools and four bins for bulk materials. Space at left for storing large tools and garden furniture. Owners: Mr. and Mrs. Bert Jastram, Oakland. Landscape architects: Eckbo, Royston, & Williams

weight on a level surface; it will be less likely to warp when in place.

Galvanized or aluminum sheet metal. Smooth surface easy to care for. *Asbestos board.* Support it well or it will break under sharp impact. *Quarry tile.* This is relatively expensive but makes a good looking permanent work top.

Flooring materials. These have all proved their worth; they're listed in order of cost: *Brick.* It looks well in the garden, water drains off it when set in sand, but it may get mossy and slick in a wet climate. *Concrete.* Easy to clean, must be well drained or water will stand in puddles. *Gravel.* Although it drains well it kicks up, a thick layer is not easy to walk on, and weeds come through. *Tanbark and sawdust.* These are least expensive but they scuff and kick up. Weeds will grow through thin layers. If not on well drained soil, they get soggy.

Three ways to build work areas in compact space

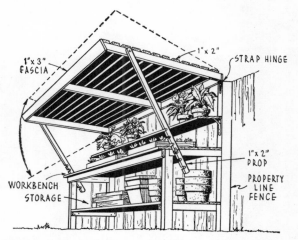

Attached to fence *workbench has lath top which hinges down to protect plants. Sheet plastic would add protection*

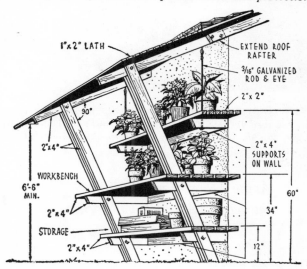

In a narrow *side yard. The lath overhead is an extension of the roof. Uprights support overhead, shelf, and workbench*

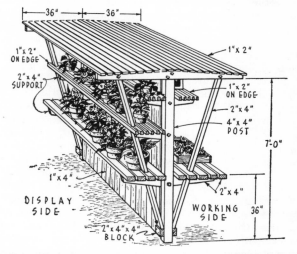

Combination freestanding *decorative screen, display area, and workbench. Face the display side toward living areas*

Work center *and shade garden (right) partially enclose the brick-paved terrace. Glass panels on south wall of the greenhouse are shaded by curtain of interlocking panels of plastic* *material on traverse rods. Same kind of curtain hangs on the west side of the shade garden. Lanai's sliding doors open onto deck. Entire glass area needs shade from south sun in summer*

At the Arboretum—Sunset Gardens in Arcadia, California

Garden work center, lanai,

This garden work center was designed for dedicated gardeners.

Located in the collector's garden in the Arboretum-*Sunset* Home Demonstration Garden in Arcadia, California, it represents the combined thinking of landscape architects Bettler Baldwin and Owen Peters, builder Harold Simpson, and *Sunset* editors who collaborated in the plans. As in the other demonstration gardens, our purpose here was to explore and experiment with new ideas in design and construction.

In a pleasant balance of practical and luxurious features, the work center includes a greenhouse for growing plants; a lanai for plant display, and for lounging in between chores; a room for potting, flower arranging, and storage of tools and garden supplies; and a small outside storage area. Directly adjoining is a garden covered with plastic shade cloth—a year-around home for many subtropicals, and a summer house for tender tropicals.

UNIQUE PANEL CONSTRUCTION

The three-unit structure (greenhouse, lanai, and workshop) is put together with a series of 4 by 8-foot panels of wood, glass, and plastic that can be built on the ground; assembled and put in place, they form the structure. The 4-foot panel width conforms with standard widths of many building materials including plywood, hardboard, and plastic materials, thus eliminating unnecessary cutting.

Using the standard size panel, you can interchange wood, glass, plastic, or any other material as the situation requires. For example, with the exception of windows in the workshop, the entire north wall of this structure is in solid plywood panels. Substitute glass for wood in any sections where you want more light. Vice versa, eliminate sun on south or west walls by using wood in place of some glass panels.

You could adopt the structure whole or in part, and scale up or down according to your needs, available space, and pocketbook.

Each panel is a structural unit framed with 2 by 3's. Posts and roof joists are required only for purposes of connection and can be lighter than usual. Here we use 1 by 4-inch uprights and 1 by 8-inch joists. See page 65 for details. If you want to build a similar structure you'd better check first with your local building department, since codes may differ.

Using 4-foot panels, you can build a greenhouse in dimensions of 4 by 8 feet, 8 by 12 feet, 8 by 16 feet, and so on, and a workshop of similar size (or smaller) according to your requirements.

At the arboretum, we decided to build three 12 by 12-foot units in which we could demonstrate the varied activities of an all-out gardener.

ROOFING

The greenhouse and lanai are roofed with 4 by 16-foot plastic covered panels with

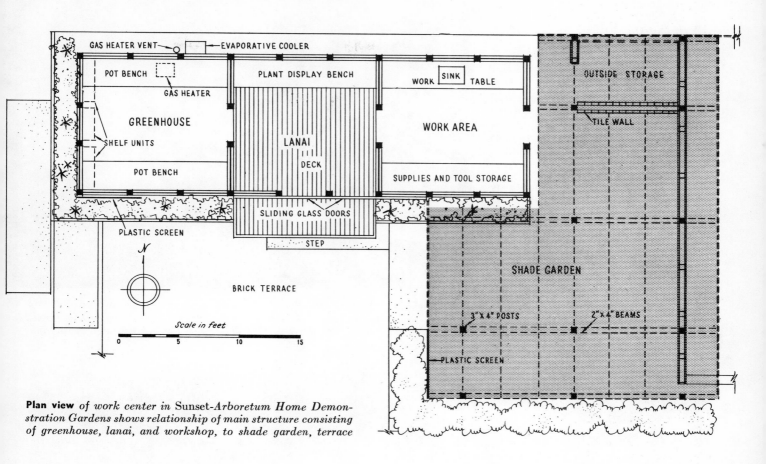

GAS HEATER VENT · EVAPORATIVE COOLER

POT BENCH

GAS HEATER

GREENHOUSE

SHELF UNITS

POT BENCH

PLASTIC SCREEN

PLANT DISPLAY BENCH

LANAI

DECK

SLIDING GLASS DOORS

STEP

WORK SINK TABLE

WORK AREA

SUPPLIES AND TOOL STORAGE

OUTSIDE STORAGE

TILE WALL

SHADE GARDEN

3" X 4" POSTS   2" X 4" BEAMS

PLASTIC SCREEN

N

Scale in feet
0   5   10   15

BRICK TERRACE

Plan view *of work center in* Sunset-*Arboretum Home Demonstration Gardens shows relationship of main structure consisting of greenhouse, lanai, and workshop, to shade garden, terrace*

and greenhouse . . . all in 4-foot panel units

a 20-inch overhang on each side. Panel frames are pulled up to the 1 by 8 joist with carriage bolts, and sealed with a foam-type weatherstripping. To prevent leaking, all joints of wood-to-wood or wood-to-plastic are sealed with a caulking compound.

The workshop is roofed with 4 by 16-foot panels of plywood surfaced with resin-impregnated wood fiber. All roof panels have 2 by 6-inch frames, tapered to provide pitch to carry rain water out to the eave line. Since the roof leaked in some sections one winter, we recommend framing the panels with 2 by 8's, thus permitting greater pitch. If you make this change, use a 1 by 10-inch joist.

During the warm months, a sheet of saran shade cloth (see page 96), which cuts out about 50 per cent sun, was stretched over the greenhouse and lanai roof. The material was stapled to 1 by 2 bats on either end of the roof and nailed to rafters on both sides. To allow for slight (1 per cent)

Shade cloth *over the top and two sides of the shade garden creates diffused light that is favorable for growing tropical and subtropical plants, pleasant for people. The structure is supported by 3 by 4 posts; 2 by 4 beams and 2 by 3 rafters overhead*

Arboretum
work center . . .

shrinkage, we left a few extra inches all around, and took up the slack by turning over the 1 by 2's at the ends and folding under the edge on the sides. We removed the material during the winter months.

FLOORING

The greenhouse and workshop floors are paved with standard 24-inch-square precast concrete pads laid on a base of 1 inch of gravel covered with 2 inches of sand. To make similar pads, line 2 by 4-inch frames with polyethylene plastic arranged loosely so as to produce a wrinkled pattern, then pour the concrete. To get the same color as in this floor, mix charcoal color with the concrete.

Easiest way to clean this floor is to hose it off, letting water drain into spaces be-

Garden books *and flower arrangement containers and accessories are kept at this end of the workshop bench. Sink and water are close by. Insecticides and fungicides are stored safely out of reach of children, in the cabinet above the sink*

Lanai *is simplified version of once-fashionable plant conservatory. Here, gardener can display his choice plants, and take time out for reading or a siesta. Decking makes it possible to hose off floor and benches, keep atmosphere cool and moist. Seen on display here are azaleas, dieffenbachias, ferns, and ficus. Plants out of bloom can be stored under the bench*

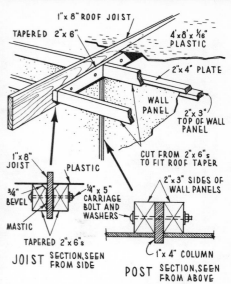

Typical roof section *shows how two roof panels are joined at a joist. Note how beveled 2 by 6 provides pitch for drainage*

At other end of *workshop bench is putterer's corner. Soil, sand, and peat moss stored in large pots under bench. Open-patterned wall outside is built with small masonry units that fit together to form a screen. It separates shade garden from storage area*

tween the pads. If you install a solid concrete floor, provide for drainage by allowing a pitch to the door or a floor drain.

The lanai has a wood deck of 2 by 3's that extends beyond the floor-to-ceiling sliding doors and wall to form an outside porch and additional display space.

COOLING SYSTEM

To cool the greenhouse we installed an evaporative cooler. This unit consists of a blower with a ¼-horsepower motor, excelsior (aspen) pads, float valve kit, and pump which distributes water over the pads on three sides of the unit, dis-

charging cool moist air into the greenhouse—and from there through automatic back-draft dampers into the lanai.

HEATING

The greenhouse is heated with an automatic vented natural gas heater that is 25 inches high and 15 inches in diameter. It is placed under the bench with the front of the heater flush with the front of the bench. In this case, the vent runs from the back of the heater outside and up the rear wall of the greenhouse. In most installations, it runs from the back of the heater vertically through the roof.

Evaporative *cooler on the rear wall delivers cool moist air into the greenhouse. On the right is a vent for the gas heater*

Each type of tool—*large, small, powered—has own niche on wall opposite flower arrangement bench. Spray equipment, watering devices on shelf above; pots, flats, other supplies, left*

Automatic mist spray *showers flats of cuttings in polyethylene film-covered frame in corner of the greenhouse. Frame is open in front. The bench is 24 inches wide, made of 1 by 3's*

Storage for tools and supplies in section at left with roof of translucent plastic. Growing center at right is protected by lath (⅜ by 2-inch redwood) on top and sides

A gardener's garden house

Part open, and part closed to provide rainproof storage, this garden house makes a good working model for the kind of outdoor structure many Westerners could use.

Landscape Architect Floyd Mick designed it for a spot at the edge of the Van W. Rosendahl garden in Piedmont, California.

But other garden locations might suit you better. You might, for example, adapt it as a dining shelter near your house. You might prefer other covering materials—perhaps solid roof with a skylight over your storage center, a greenhouse instead of a lathhouse over your potted plants.

Outdoor potting bench, protected by lath, is also good spot for bringing potted plants into bloom for display. Some might make this also the display center, facing it toward the house

Bench for work, or seedling flats. Plastic roof diffuses the light and keeps out rain, cuts sun's intensity. Tools stored at right

Looking toward house through breezeway between lath and tool storage sections. Plastic roof extends over the passageway

Bins for soil, fertilizer, potting mixes stored under counters, can be moved easily on their rubber-tired dolly wheels

Lathhouse interior. Bench goes all the way around, then doubles back along lath partition to give an extra dividend of working space. Surface, 36 inches above floor, is a convenient height when standing and working with pots and flats. Note that the width is ample to accommodate a flat. Concrete slab floor under the whole unit. Pitched roof adapts to greenhouse combination

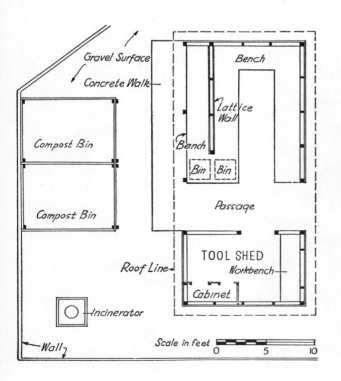

Gravel Surface
Concrete Walk
Compost Bin
Compost Bin
Roof Line
Incinerator
Wall
Scale in feet
0 5 10

Bench
Lattice Wall
Bench
Bin Bin
Passage
TOOL SHED
Workbench
Cabinet

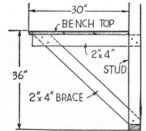

30"
BENCH TOP
2"x 4" STUD
36"
2"x 4" BRACE

Counters. *Diagonal brace support for plenty of leg room. Boards spaced for drainage*

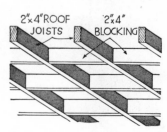

24" 24"
2"x 2"
28"

Bins. *Use sheet metal to line, and to cover part of counter directly over for rainproofing*

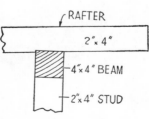

RAFTER
2"x 4"
4"x 4" BEAM
2"x 4" STUD

Rafters. *Of 2 by 4's notched, carried by 4 by 4 beams across 4 by 4 posts and 2 by 4 studs*

2"x 4" ROOF JOISTS
2"x 4" BLOCKING

Blocking. *Spacers are 2 by 4. Lumber of this dimension is enough to support light roof*

Potting center is located along street side of the garden. Gate at far left is convenient for truck delivery of heavy materials

Work centers for the pot gardener

A planned work center, no matter how simple, will add to your gardening pleasure. In the potting center above, the aluminum sink and plastic covered counter are used also for salad making when meals are served in the barbecue area nearby. Fertilizers and potting mixes are kept in closed cabinets under the counter.

The work area below consists of portable units which provide all the essentials for any small potting center.

Bins for leaf mold, manure, and potting mixes could be protected from rain by a canvas drop, mounted on a ½-inch dowel, and tacked to the table edge above. Note the convenient towel rack on the far left unit.

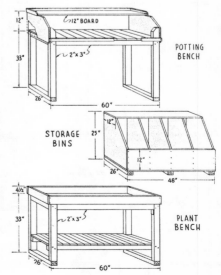

Start with one of these units, build on as your gardening experiences expand. Tray table for flats and pot storage, work table with space below for bins

Simple and versatile design idea

There is no such thing as the *perfect* work center. No two gardeners have the same interests; also, the difference between the beginner and the experienced gardener isn't measured in degrees of completeness.

For example, a gardener who specializes in begonias may have no interest in a complete garden of shrubs, trees, and flowers. The development of a gardener from an unwilling pusher of a lawn mower doesn't proceed in an orderly fashion. The reluctant gardener of today may be the orchid grower of tomorrow After years of watching Western gardeners at work and play, we feel that the real need is for a work center plan that will be as expandable as the interest of the gardener — sufficiently adaptable to changes in direction to take care of the changing whims of the gardener.

The L-wall

One basic device is an L-wall. With this, you have at least a place to hang things, to pile things, to hide things, and shelter from wind. You can locate such a unit in a small garden so

JOHN ROBINSON

With a portion of the unit roofed over, garden center becomes all-weather work shop and shelter for seed flats and equipment

that it is a part of the garden design. Such an L-wall will give you a place to take care of materials brought in for occasional splurges of work, such as annual lawn treatment, brick laying, or concrete work.

Even such occasional use suggests the addition of some type of a roof. And, of course, the roof would be followed by a work bench, and storage of some type, whether gardening is basic or complicated.

When your gardening includes growing plants from seed, transplanting, and pot gardening, a long list of materials enter your life. There must be containers for leaf mold, peat, vermiculite, sand, and loam; flats to use and store. There are many ways to store sand and like materials. Bins look more efficient, but when loaded with sand or soil they are heavy and hard to swing open. Suggested here are garbage pails. They keep the materials dry, do not rust, and they can be rolled into position for use or filling.

L-wall fits in many situations, can be oriented to sun and wind

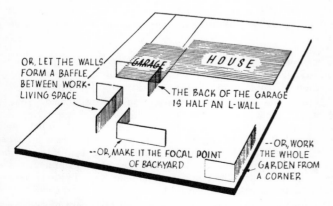

OR, LET THE WALLS FORM A BAFFLE BETWEEN WORK-LIVING SPACE

GARAGE · HOUSE

THE BACK OF THE GARAGE IS HALF AN L-WALL

--OR, MAKE IT THE FOCAL POINT OF BACKYARD

--OR, WORK THE WHOLE GARDEN FROM A CORNER

Starting with simple L-wall, gardener can add type of work and storage units required, keep them concentrated in one area

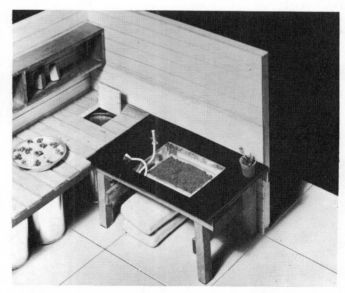

Sink opening should be large enough for standard 15 by 23-inch flat. A faucet with spray attachment will always come in handy

If there are flats and pots, a sink is a valuable asset to the work center. It should be large enough to take a standard flat for bottom soaking. Note the suggestion of a hole in bench for waste disposal into garbage can. **Turn page for more ideas**

Cold frames and lath frame for protection of seedlings, storage bins for soil, soil conditioners, brought together in one unit

If you get into volume production with seedlings and transplants, you will find that containers in which you can work with a long handle shovel are more efficient than cans or barrels. Take, for example, the twin purpose unit illustrated above. It will accommodate four flats of seedlings in various stages of growth. Bins of peat moss, sand, leaf mold, fertilizer are close at hand for mixing.

For ruggedness, two-inch redwood stock is recommended for the sides of the bins, with sheet metal facing over the back to withstand the constant denting of shovels. A smooth concrete bottom is desirable.

In soil mixing, a square of smooth concrete paving is the best mixing surface. You can mix materials on it with a shovel and then hose off the remnants when you are finished. You'll get adequate drainage with a pitch of one-quarter-inch to the foot.

Sooner or later, as gardening operations become more varied, you will not wish to continue buying everything in small quantities. Peat moss by the bale and fertilizer by the 100 pound sack are cheaper than by the package. And, sooner or later, the

garage will bulge at the seams with materials that must be kept dry. A tool and storage shed can be added to appear as a part of the work center. Unit at left, below, is built against a short wall of the "L" with construction matching the basic unit. For the sake of appearance, or as a further wind screen, it could become a third wall. Plain sliding doors are the most practical because they won't swing in the wind, need no latches.

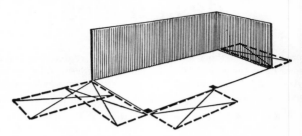

There are no fixed positions for any of work center units. Above are 4 positions for storage unit in connection with L-wall

Before increasing either storage or working space let's check on what storage and equipment we have for what gardener.

The "I'll-keep-mine-simple" type gardener can use the simple L-wall to good advantage. It gives him a storage place for many things.

The addition of storage for soil conditioners and the work areas for flats takes care of the gardener growing plants from seeds.

Protected storage locker relieves the garage of the accumulation resulting from intensive gardening.

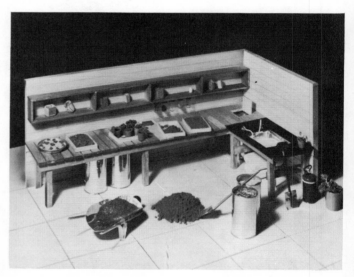

Example of a unit developed by a gardener whose activities include growing from seed and cuttings, potting, and spraying

The compost pile, the trash burner, or burning pit can be added to the unit by either above-ground units or in pits. Remember that compost piles need aeration for rapid decay.

Above is one way the work center could be organized. Roof is removed for a better view. The possibilities of improving the efficiency in such an area as this are endless. Seeds, labels, and other small articles can be stored in matching jars or cans. Without much effort a flower arrangement center could be added. All small tools should be conveniently at hand. A cabinet for spray and dust materials should be provided. Again, how far to go is determined by the activities of the gardener.

The unit as developed to this point will take care of everyone except the specialist, who must have winter protection; or the

Main roof is extended slightly to protect join. Sliding doors require no latching, and make it easy to get to heavy equipment

gardener who is tackling plant material which is difficult to propagate. The germination of seeds and the rooting of cuttings are speeded up by "bottom heat" in the form of warm soil. If your gardening calls for the handling of hard-to-root cuttings, some form of controlled heat is essential. Such heat can be furnished by soil-heating cable in a small cutting box, such as illustrated below. In this example we have placed a lath-covered unit for transplanted seedlings alongside the cutting box. Cutting boxes are closed so that humidity can be increased.

Greenhouse might be a lean-to attached to wall of south exposure. Conventional type standing alone receives more light

If your program does not call for a greenhouse, a simple box on the work bench will take care of propagation by cuttings

A small lean-to of type above is not expensive to build, but it has limitations. It must have southern exposure on account of the solid wall. This fact may complicate the placement of the L-wall for other factors such as prevailing winds. A conventional type greenhouse could be placed in position on the open side of the wall and at the same time give a better flow to the work.

The important thing to remember in your planning is that each operation in the garden has corresponding work center needs. You'll be happier if you plan for the possibility of expansion.

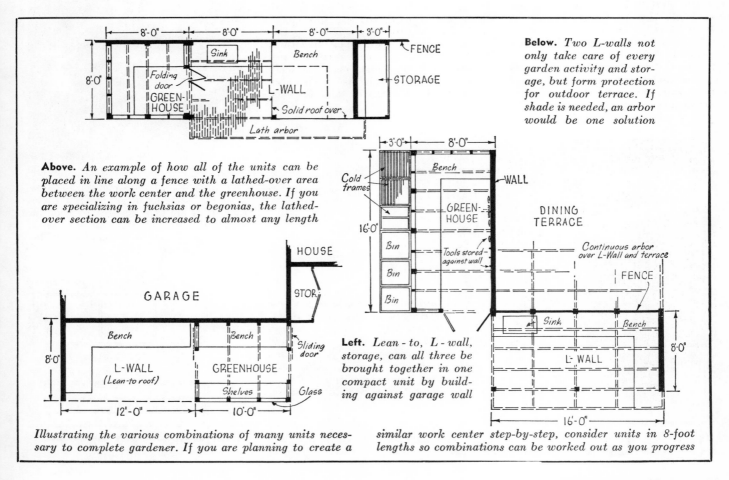

Below. *Two L-walls not only take care of every garden activity and storage, but form protection for outdoor terrace. If shade is needed, an arbor would be one solution*

Above. *An example of how all of the units can be placed in line along a fence with a lathed-over area between the work center and the greenhouse. If you are specializing in fuchsias or begonias, the lathed-over section can be increased to almost any length*

Left. *Lean-to, L-wall, storage, can all three be brought together in one compact unit by building against garage wall*

Illustrating the various combinations of many units necessary to complete gardener. If you are planning to create a

similar work center step-by-step, consider units in 8-foot lengths so combinations can be worked out as you progress

Why try to hide it?

On casual display in a center like this, the equipment of the working gardener can be just as attractive as the hanging array of pots and pans which brighten a kitchen

POT AND FLAT RACK. This sturdy showcase could hold even large tubs. Top boards are spaced a little for direct drainage from containers to the floor. The rack can be moved around easily. By altering design only slightly and adding another tier, you could increase its capacity to fit your garden needs.

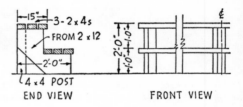

WHEN YOU genuinely like to garden, should you hide the obvious evidence? The R. B. MacBrides of Modesto, California, do not think so. In their garden, designed by Landscape Architect Thomas Church, they give their garden work center a prominent corner in full view of the outdoor living area. Here are some of its features.

WORK TABLE. On its broad top, backed by a splash board, you can mix quantities of potting soil with a shovel. If the wood has a seal coat, clean off with a hose. Lower storage space is ample; toe space is good. Some might move the shelf back to give more shin space. This also could double as a service table for outdoor parties.

SOIL BINS. Each compartment holds almost five sackfuls of garden raw materials. Bins are kept rot-free by good air circulation beneath. With all tops down, the whole structure becomes a garden bench or handy counter.

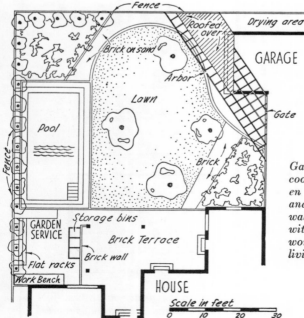

Gardening can be as sociable as cooking becomes when the kitchen has loafing space for family and visitors. Only a low brick wall, hiding just the soil bins with tops down, separates this work center from main outdoor living terrace next to the house

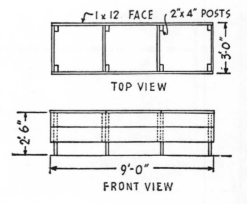

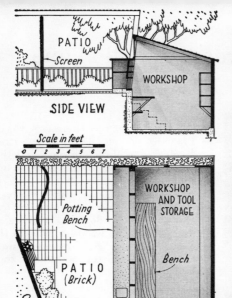

SIDE VIEW

Scale in feet
0 1 2 3 4 5 6 7

Potting Bench

PATIO (Brick)

CAR PORT

WORKSHOP AND TOOL STORAGE

Bench

DN.

PLAN VIEW

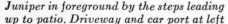

Juniper in foreground by the steps leading up to patio. Driveway and car port at left

Potting bench at side of work center. Lath overhead extends left to car port. Obscure glass lets light into the workshop at right. Note hose storage in the foreground

Planned to fit a hillside site

This compact garden work center fits snugly against the slope that runs along one side of a small patio.

From the street it is easily reached by steps. Its location near the car port is particularly convenient for bringing in garden supplies by auto.

Tool storage and workshop are located on the downhill side, with potting bench at patio level. There is waterproof storage space under the bench on a concrete slab. The work center is joined to the car port by an overhead lath shelter.

Architect Harvey Harwood of Los Angeles designed the work center for his own garden.

LEFT. *High windows over the bench let in light through uphill side of workshop*

ABOVE. *A small concrete bench opposite main work center juts from car port wall. It is convenient for potting or display*

Work center, plant display, garden room . . . all in one

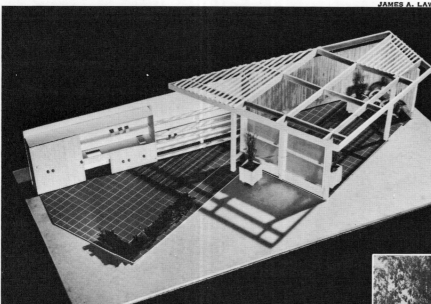

JAMES A. LAWRENCE

Landscape Architect Douglas Baylis of San Francisco presents here with one structure a solution to three problems and thereby has created an interesting example for gardeners everywhere to follow.

The three problems which received his consideration were — one, a work center; two, a display of flowers; and three, a garden room. The important thing is that in a small garden these three needs are often encountered and can be brought together into one unit.

Interesting, too, is the method by which adequate garden color is obtained with but very little planting and soil. Pots and tubs and a vine or two make a garden out of these two rooms.

The design was checked by building a model. Certain minor faults came to light in model construction—the need to carry roof line above garden wall, for example. Comparing photographs of unit to model proves model's value as a mirror of the future building

The glass used in partition separating the two rooms and acting as a windbreak has rough surface, is less expensive to use than a polished glass. The glass panes shown here measure 3 by 5 feet

JOHN ROBINSON

The fence is a new type of woven-wire, Western split cedar and is 6 feet high. Out of the 600 square feet allowed for the garden, 500 are paved. The greater the paved area, the more living space

Work bench and tool and supply storage are simply done. Darker paint would prove more serviceable. Pot rack is well spaced, giving the Darwin dahlias a chance to display themselves properly

At the left, sink, potting bench; soil bins underneath. At right, work bench, tools

Glass-top potting shed

A glass-over-lath roof gives this six by nine-foot combination potting shed and workshop good natural daylight for work and enough sunlight for some forms of propagation. The design was by Harwell Hamilton Harris.

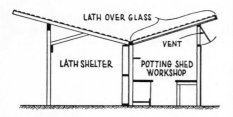

Cross section of potting shed-workshop shows how it joins a lath plant shelter

Two high panels swing out for ventilation

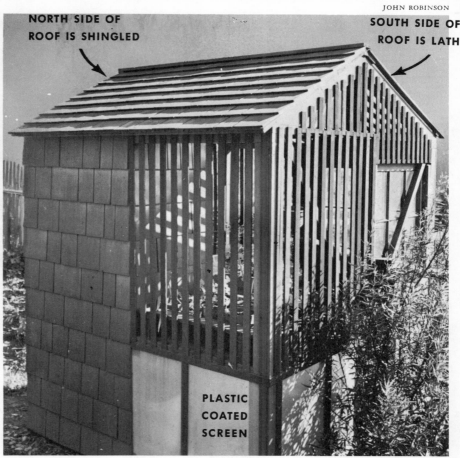

NORTH SIDE OF ROOF IS SHINGLED

SOUTH SIDE OF ROOF IS LATH

PLASTIC COATED SCREEN

This all-purpose garden workshop provides a variety of controlled weather conditions. Materials are standard-sized, inexpensive. Owner: Colonel Miles Kresge, Berkeley

36 square feet of work space

We've seen home owners get so carried away with the idea of a garden workshop that they make it much too elaborate for their needs. We've seen others who think only in terms of large nursery installations—which they can't afford—so they never have a garden work center at all.

In many Western home gardens, the best compromise is a small, inexpensive structure like the one above. Designed for the climatic conditions prevailing in the Berkeley hills, it serves as both greenhouse and lathhouse. To avoid waste, dimensions were based on standard lengths and sizes of materials.

On the side walls, below the workbench, plastic-coated screen lets in the sun, keeps out the wind and weather, and provides hothouse conditions. This area is ideal for propagating cuttings, wintering some plants, and seeding others. Pots are sunk into the tanbark area, and the adjacent sand well merely holds a reserve supply for cuttings.

Above the bench the owner has provided lathhouse conditions, with one corner protected from the prevailing wind by clear glass windows. He can move pots and

flats around on the bench in order to protect tender plants during the colder weather. A portable glass frame for germinating seeds fits on the bench nearest the doorway. Ample, protected storage is provided in the cabinet at the right of the door.

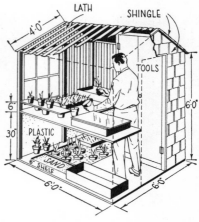

Within the small three-foot floor area you can stand or kneel to reach any tray or shelf in this compact little structure

APLIN-DUDLEY STUDIO

Potting, storage area looking toward front part of garden. Pink and tan flagstone used in floor and lower part of wall. Redwood grapestakes top wall. Overlapping glass panes overhead. Wire glass adds extra protection on the two end walls

Attached to house, across from potting bench, is storage cabinet and counter. It can be used for pot display, arranging flowers or for extra working space. It is made of the same stone as house

Putterer's corner
. . . efficient and pleasant

In a narrow space on the west side of their house, Mr. and Mrs. Harry Eichelberger, Jr., Santa Monica, California, have built a garden work center. It serves as a model for the gardener with a strong yen for puttering and a feeling for display. Protected from wind and sun on all sides, it has a complete and compact set-up for potting and seed sowing, and garden storage. Pot shelves and hanging baskets add a conservatory touch. Mildred Davis, garden consultant.

Pot shelves of begonias, fuchsias, campanulas, ivies make a colorful wall at lower end of work center. Rear garden beyond

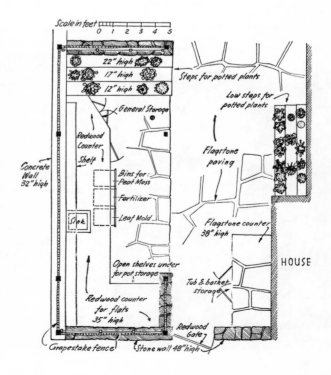

Scale in feet 0 1 2 3 4 5

22" high
17" high
12" high

Steps for potted plants

General Storage

Low steps for potted plants

Redwood Counter Shelf

Concrete Wall 32" high

Bins for:
Peat Moss
Fertilizer
Leaf Mold

Flagstone paving

Sink

Flagstone counter 38" high

HOUSE

Open shelves under for pot storage

Tub & basket storage

Redwood counter for flats 35" high

Redwood Gate

Grapestake fence

Stone wall 48" high

Split bamboo fence *and the seat wall have been extended from the patio (to left) along the side of the greenhouse to integrate the two sections of the garden. Raised brick platform between the greenhouse and lathhouse further extends line of seat wall*

Unity in design . . . with split bamboo

The elegant appearance of this garden work center developed out of an existing split bamboo fence.

Originally, the fence ran along one side of the patio, which is located to the left of the greenhouse in the photograph above. Later the bamboo was extended as a veneer over the walls of the greenhouse and lathhouse. Split bamboo also covers the top of the lathhouse.

The result is an attractive unity about the entire area as seen from the house and patio.

The split bamboo was attached to a board backing with brass screws driven through holes drilled in the bamboo (nails split bamboo). You can now buy woven fencing of split or round natural bamboo in the following sizes: (split) 16 by 25 feet, 6 by 18 feet, and 4 by 25 feet; (round natural) 6 by 25 feet.

Owners are Mr. and Mrs. Herbert Dean, Pebble Beach, California. Architect is Jon Koningshofer, Carmel, California.

Lathhouse *facing greenhouse seen above is used mostly for growing cymbidiums. Split bamboo is attached to a board backing. Glass under roof on side of lathhouse facing the garden. Floor is paved with brick. Clipped privet hedge grows along the side*

All-purpose storage unit for a compact

The two combined units of this garden work center provide space for all gardening equipment with room for paint and tool locker. Fold-down door provides extra counter adjacent to work bench. A service yard paved with concrete makes this a year-around, all-purpose work area. Construction details are shown below. Use 90-pound mineral surface roll roofing. Warm it first to room temperature to avoid cracking, then bend it over the top edge of the storage unit and nail on the drip molding

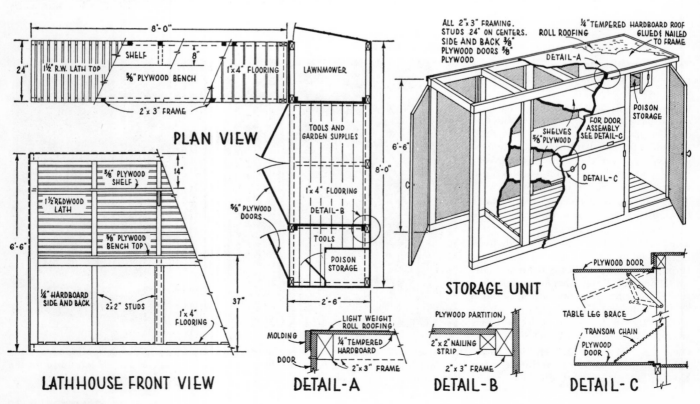

garden work center

If you are like most home owners, you have had garden storage problems—where to store your lawnmower? where to hang your rake and spade? where to keep a bale of peat moss, a bag of manure, or any of the garden paraphernalia you work with? Here is one possible solution.

We combined a small lathhouse and potting bench with an all-purpose storage unit, designed especially to fit the needs of those who have no garage or basement storage space. The two units will give you a place to store all your essential garden tools and materials, plus a workbench with a shelf for some of your shade loving plants. Materials for the entire work center will cost about $125.

End section for lawnmower built with no flooring; lawnmower rolls in without lifting. Other lawn tools hang on side walls. There is space at the top for an extra shelf if needed. Small tubular locks can be installed on any doors for security

Test model was located in side yard service area, close to door into house, screened from street by existing basket weave fence

By placing these two units so that they form an L, you might screen off your service yard, a woodpile, garbage cans, or any unsightly nominations for the junkyard.

You can change the exterior materials or alter the dimensions to fit any location in your yard, and you can add to or subtract from any features of our model. If you like to have running water right where you are working, obtain a used sink, cut a hole in the workbench top, fit in the sink, and attach the faucet to a convenient garden hose. If the concrete slab you use is perfectly smooth, perhaps you'll want to replace the garbage can we used with simple plywood bins on rubber casters.

From the garden side, work center screens drying yard and woodpile behind. Clematis Armandii on 1 by 1 and 2 by 2-inch redwood trellis with No. 10 wire and galvanized screw eyes. Lath section stained to match house siding and redwood fence

ALTERNATE SUGGESTIONS FOR LOCATION OF WORK CENTER

Before you start building, check on your local zoning ordinances to see how close to a side or rear yard fence you may place these units. In many locations you can put a structure anywhere you want as long as you don't anchor it to the ground or a concrete slab. In other areas you may find that you must abide by requirements governing detached structures in side or rear yards.

If you use plywood, make certain that it is exterior grade material. Give it a good primer coat, using either resin sealer or paint primer. Finish with a coat of exterior house paint in a color to harmonize with your house or fence. Be sure to use several coats of the primer on any exposed plywood edges.

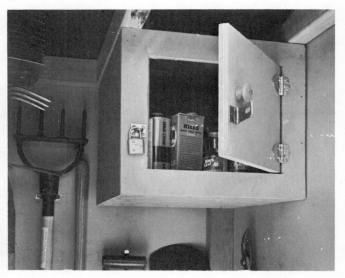

Padlocked chest provides out-of-reach storage for poison garden sprays, pest baits. Spring clamps convenient for garden tools

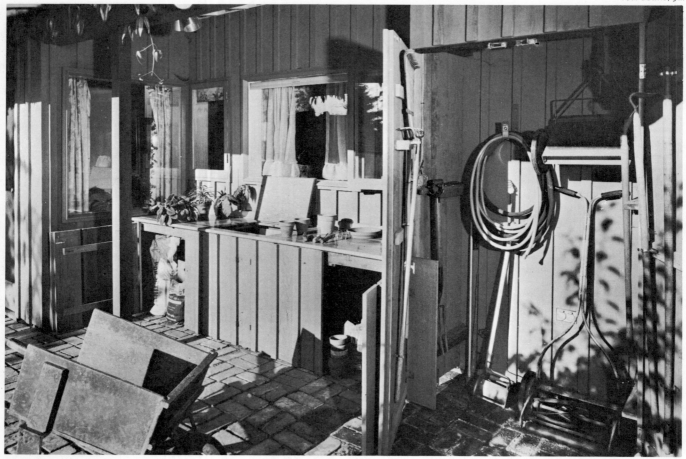

Efficient work center has two large cupboards for storing fertilizers and flower pots; a covered sink; a closet for mower, larger tools

Here is sensible tool storage

This garden work center is conveniently close to both house and garden. Located on the house wall outside a bedroom and study, it faces the flower beds across the brick patio.

Tools and supplies are well concealed when the work center is not in use. A hinged lid covers the sink opening. There is generous storage space for both large and small items under the maple counter and in the tool closet at the right. The closet also has a hose connection and two electric outlets.

There are certain advantages to locating the work center and storage area next to the house: Here are a few:

1) Less lumber and labor is necessary, because the house serves as one wall.

2) A work center can easily double as a flower arranging center when it is only a few steps from the house.

3) If the work center is located under the patio overhead, it can be used in cold or rainy weather.

The architect was Jack Stafford, of Eugene, Oregon.

With all the doors closed, *work center is inconspicuous in a jog in the house wall. Cedar siding below counter is same material as the house. Battens used as door pulls*

Dual-purpose storage wall serves as fence for patio and as a place to put pots, tools, fertilizers and other garden equipment

A storage wall
in the patio

Storage space is welcome any place, but often it is omitted in the patio and in the garden.

For Architect Harold Eckman's home in Tucson, Arizona, some type of screen was needed between patio and adjacent driveway. The wall, shown in the plan below, provides privacy for patio dining and entertaining. At the same time it supplies storage space on the patio side where it is most needed.

Roofed corner *of enclosed service yard protects tools hung on wall. Canvas drop cloth, open in summer, is closed for winter protection. Owners: Mr. and Mrs. Isidore Schuman, Woodside, California. Architects: Wurster, Bernardi & Emmons*

Two garden storage shelters

Since the tendency of most gardeners is to keep all tools—and add more as better or more intriguing ones come on the market—they have a continuous storage problem.

The picture above shows an easy-to-build inexpensive shelter for tools and equipment of many shapes and sizes. Below is a storage "cave" set into a garden wall.

Here are some points to keep in mind about garden storage: Allow enough floor

Opening *for storage in concrete wall at M. D. Skroopka garden in West Los Angeles. Doors are plywood. Landscape architects: Eckbo, Royston & Williams*

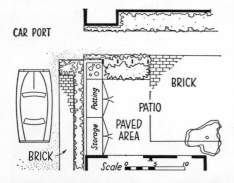

Storage wall, seen from driveway, is a screen for patio. One by two-inch boards nailed on fence make nice shadow pattern

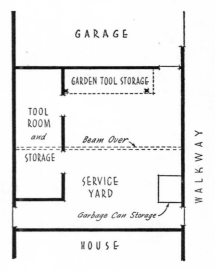

space to accommodate bulky items like wheelbarrows and power mowers. Make use of all surfaces; a surprising number of items, like the buckets in the photograph above, can be hung overhead. Put storage as near the point of use as you can. Notice in the picture on the left, how the fertilizer and other such materials are right in the garden. A storage space near the driveway is always desirable for bulky materials.

Storage next to the house

Faced with the problem of too little space for too much equipment, John A. Eliot of Santa Barbara, California, took a look at the wide roof overhang shielding his paved side yard. Here he had protection from rain and a ready-built floor—a good start toward a convenient storage cabinet.

Construction was kept simple. The cabinet has a 2 by 4-inch frame bolted to the concrete. It is sheathed with fixed panels and hinged doors made of 1-inch redwood planks. A roof of ¾-inch plywood supplies necessary bracing. Wood blocks nailed to the concrete keep wheeled equipment from rolling out on the sloping pavement through open doors.

If you don't have a roof overhang, you could weatherproof a similar cabinet with roll roofing. If you don't want the cabinet next to the house, it could be free standing and function as a screen, or it could use a fence as one wall.

WILLIAM APLIN

Two lawnmowers, *a wheelbarrow, garden spray equipment, long-handled brooms, brushes, and tools all fit beneath eaves*

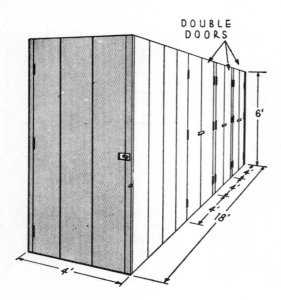

Walls of cabinet *are made of 1-inch redwood planks, finished with a clear spar-type varnish. Ordinary hasps serve as handles*

Storage beneath the house

Here is a good way to use the space underneath a one-level, hillside house. Very little work was needed to convert it into a dirt-floored storage room. A dense screen of vines hides the storage room from the lower garden and patio, and also gives the downhill side of the house a handsome façade.

MORLEY BAER

House and deck *seem to "float" over evergreen vines, which camouflage the storage room behind. Architect was John Funk*

Storage area below house *is protected from wind and rain. It could be closed in later if added living space were required*

Portable storage

*Also on this page . . . an
easy-to-make potter's seat*

Storage on wheels offers excellent possibilities, especially for gardens that have generous amounts of paving to accommodate the rolling stock. Here we offer an example of such a carryall. One interesting variation that could be made: a three-sided version with no storage inside and no door, for those who do not care about the storage space for insecticides and fertilizers.

Both the carryall and the potter's seat shown on this page were invented by gardening enthusiasts who had the same basic thought in mind: to make gardening easier.

GARDEN CARRYALL

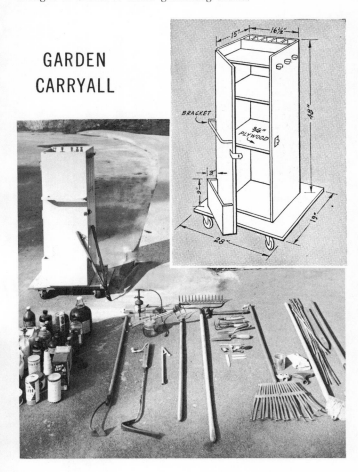

Cart, designed for a garden with walks and ramps, holds long-handled tools around outside, small hand tools, sprinklers in compartments at top, sprays and plant foods on shelves inside

Capacity is about six cubic feet. Poisons kept locked inside. Cart designed by Mrs. J. R. Osherenko, Beverly Hills, Calif.

Potter's seat of wood for resting while moving seedlings from flats to pots. Slide at right holds empty pots in neat order

POTTER'S SEAT

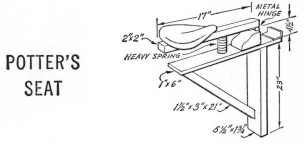

If bicycle seat were substituted, heavy spring could be eliminated. Devised by Peter Riedel, Santa Barbara, California

The deep sink *is a comfortable height for flower arranging. Pots, bowls, and containers are handy in the cupboard below*

Flower arranging center in a passageway

This work center, in a passageway between the car port and kitchen, is efficiently arranged in a handy place and easy to keep looking neat and clean.

It is used for flower arranging, tool storage, and storage of produce from the nearby garden. Owners: Mr. and Mrs. Elon Gilbert, Yakima, Washington. Architect: Thomas F. Hargis, Jr.

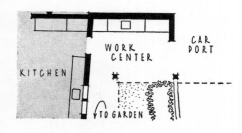

The tall cabinet *near the kitchen door is for fruit and vegetables. Other tall cabinet (in foreground) is for the lawnmower and garden tools. Work counter and sink between*

Adding cheer and color to the side yard

This side yard between house and car port has become a cheerful flower arranging center and service area. It is readily accessible from the kitchen, car port, and front and rear garden. Back of the car port is a storage room. The floor is of burnt adobe brick, same material as that used for the house. Contrasting with the reddish brick are soft blue canvas awnings that can be stretched on wires to form a ramada.

CLYDE CHILDRESS

Cabinet *holds containers and accessories for flower arranging. Owners are Mr. and Mrs. G. Harold Pfau, Tucson, Arizona*

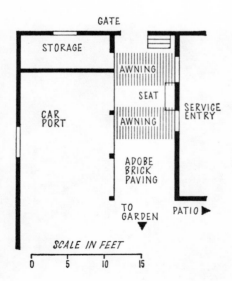

Plan *shows relationship to house, grounds. A gate—not visible in photo—can close off all but top one-quarter of doorway*

Patio headquarters for flower arranging

One of the best ways to get the clutter of flower arranging out of the kitchen is to provide a special place for this job on the patio. All you need is a counter, a sink and faucet, and storage for tools, bowls, and vases. If you have a vegetable garden, you can also use this area when you clean and top the vegetables. Here we show two examples: a large area against a fence, and a compact work center next to the house.

JULIUS SHULMAN

Garden fence *forms back of the storage cabinets. Sink in the small counter has a faucet with a gooseneck spout. The design was by landscape architects Eckbo, Royston & Williams*

RUSSELL ILLIG

Arrangement center *at Sunset headquarters in Menlo Park, California, has counters to match patio tile. Area is 10 feet wide; narrower version would do for average sized home*

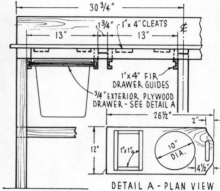

End view *of the bench shows the simple construction of the frame. If desired, you could add a shelf on the lower support*

30¾"

1¾" | 1"x 4" CLEATS
13" | 13"

1"x 4" FIR DRAWER GUIDES
¾" EXTERIOR PLYWOOD DRAWER - SEE DETAIL A

26½" 2"

12" 1"x1" 10" DIA. 4½"

DETAIL A - PLAN VIEW

This compact potting bench *is just about the right size to fit into the work center of the average sized home garden. The four gaily colored plastic pails, dropped through holes in pull-out shelves, contain peat moss, leaf mold, sand, and perlite*

Half-view *of the front elevation of bench shows how pails are suspended. Can use a different colored pail for each material*

A dozen pieces of useful garden equipment . . . all easy to build

To aid the expert

DARROW M. WATT

Are you interested in becoming a better gardenkeeper? Are you handy with tools? Do you like to make things yourself? If so, you'll be interested in the gardener's items shown here and on two following pages.

These are practical, workable, useful pieces of equipment—call some of them gadgets, if you like—the sort of thing you'll find in the gardens, work centers, and potting sheds of many Western gardeners. As one explained, "They help you to be a better organized gardener."

Being well organized, by the way, needn't take the fun out of gardening. The fact is, it's the other way around. When work runs along smoothly and efficiently, when there's a place for everything and everything is in its place, you have that much more time to enjoy your garden.

If you are a putterer who likes to sow seed or pot plants, or if you're intrigued with container gardening, then the potting bench, pot display stand, rotary soil mixer and sifter, and pot rack will catch your eye. So will the row-marker for flats, the leveling board, small sifter, and dibber. For everybody who handles a bottle of spray—and this applies especially to those with small children—the little box with its lock and key is practically a must.

Top of bench, *hinged at back, lifted to show use of space behind pails for small tools, labels, and such. Front 1 by 1 partition becomes drawer stop; use 2-inch material for deeper drawer*

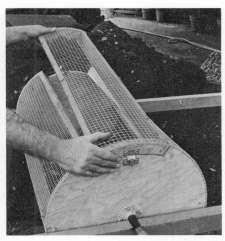

Materials *shoveled through opening made possible by removable section. Sash lock and screen hanger hold section in place*

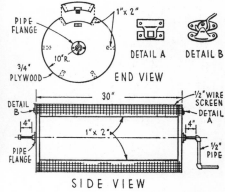

PIPE FLANGE

1" x 2"

DETAIL A

DETAIL B

3/4" PLYWOOD

10" R.

END VIEW

DETAIL B

30"

1/2" WIRE SCREEN

DETAIL A

4"

1" x 2"

4"

PIPE FLANGE

1/2" PIPE

SIDE VIEW

A 30-inch-long cylinder *of ½-inch hardware cloth on wooden frame, with plywood ends, makes sifting soil easy. If you want to mix the potting materials first, tie a piece of canvas around cylinder to keep sand and other fine ingredients from sifting through*

Detail sketch *shows construction of sifter*

gardener . . . and delight the garden putterer

Safety box for insecticides *is 12¾ by 8¾ inches and 10 inches high. Made of ½-inch plywood; room for 6 quart bottles; partitioned by ½-inch plywood. Has false bottom with holes cut to hold pint sized bottles. Measuring spoons in lid*

Box *weighs 8 pounds empty; easy to carry even when full. Hose-end sprayer fits in one section. Keep the box locked when not in use*

More easy-to-build garden equipment . . .

Most of the items that you see on this page were made in an hour or less. It would take an amateur the better part of a Saturday afternoon to make the pot display stand or the basket. A good time saver: Buy the lumber pre-cut. It's a good idea to use surfaced lumber for items you plan to handle frequently.

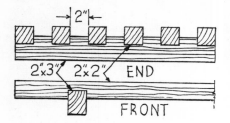

Pot display bench *placed outside a floor-to-ceiling living room window takes the place of a bed of flowers that never looked quite trim. Off the ground, potted plants are free of soil pests, splashed mud, winter dampness. See detail sketch at the left*

Easy-to-make, *stock-in-trade items for the gardener who likes to grow his own plants: flat for sowing seed, pricking out seedlings; level made of 1 by 6 wood; dibble made from dowel*

Wooden basket *of simple but attractive design for carrying plants, small garden tools, and accessories. Use 1-inch surfaced material, dowel for top of handle. Basket is sturdy, yet light*

Sifter *is made of 1 by 4-inch stock, surfaced. Bottom of ½-inch hardware cloth. Use sifter to screen small amounts of soil, leaf mold, peat moss, and other potting mix ingredients*

Small sifter *(8 inches square), with fine screen on bottom, is used to sift a covering of soil mix or sand over newly sown seeds. Also use for sifting soil over surface before sowing seed*

Lath shades *on stand of 1 by 1-inch stock form temporary miniature lathhouse over new transplants. Also useful to place over flats. Use 1 by 1-inch material for the stringers or crosspieces*

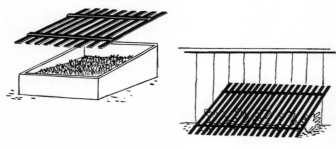

Two more ways *you can use the lath shade: Left, as a shade on top of coldframe sash; right, as a temporary lean-to over plants growing in a sunny border against a fence or wall*

The same shades, *without a stand, form a tent over rows of annuals that have just been planted out. Use common lath or better grade material. Could also use woven lath or snow fencing*

DARROW M. WATT

Row marker, *made to fit a standard flat, uses 1-inch surfaced lath beveled along bottom edge. Stamps out 10 uniform rows when pressed into soil. Good for seeding in rows, pricking out*

Pots of various sizes, *stacked neatly on 3-foot-high dowels of different diameters (depending on the sizes of the holes in pots). Dowels are anchored in holes drilled in a 2 by 12-inch plank*

cans from view, but which would also make a good simple potting bench. Garbage cans could hold potting soil or fertilizer. Spaces between the slats would allow pots or flats to drain. A wide board on top could be used for soil mixing.

Both of these potting bench devices were designed by Landscape Architects Osmundson-Staley of San Francisco.

Fence makes handy support for a projecting lath panel over a small garden work center

Redwood 1 by 2's across top. Wire mesh for vines over open fence section above

Two ideas for potting benches

Also . . . tool hangers from scrap lumber

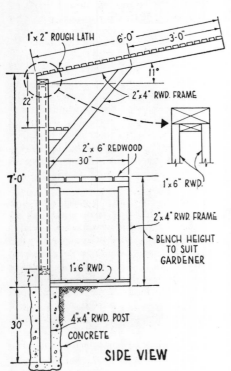

SIDE VIEW

The potting bench shown in the photo above was designed to fit behind a seven-foot screening fence. There it can easily be shielded from the house or the display areas of a garden.

The overhead shelter is lath. As a cover for shade-loving plants during the summer, the lath frame should be oriented so that the sun moves across the slats, not along their length.

For winter use, the lath frame might be projected southward to catch the full sun. Canvas over lath would give some frost protection at night. One section of the lath frame could be made into a solid roof to act as a partial rain shelter.

In the next column is another device designed originally to hide two garbage

PLAN VIEW

3" SPACING ON STAGGERED 1"x 6" RWD.

JOHN ROBINSON

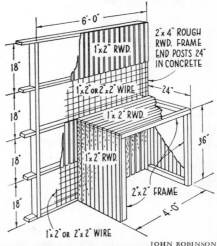

Short scrap boards can be used to make hangers which hold three garden tools against a wall or fence. Designed by Landscape Architects Litton and Whitney

New developments in composting

Somewhere in the vicinity of most garden work centers is a compost pile. It can be a nuisance; but if you know what you're doing, it is extremely worthwhile

During the past ten years, many researchers, manufacturers, and plain dirt gardeners have announced "improvements" or "advances" in the ancient art of composting. Some of these have been extremely helpful and some have been confusing or misleading. In this article we look at three main developments:

1. Compost inoculums, activators, and similar products.

2. The thoroughgoing compost research project done by the University of California's Department of Sanitary Engineering.

3. New methods and devices to make composting easier and more efficient.

First, let's take our bearings. What is compost and what is composting?

WHAT IS COMPOST?

Scrape away the coarse litter on the surface of a finished, well run compost pile; reach down elbow-deep, and grab a handful of the earthy material inside. Soft, sweet smelling, fine grained, spongy, and moist, it looks like the essence of soil fertility. It is. But the richness of compost depends on the richness of the raw ingredients used to make it. Compost made from lawn clippings and garden trash may analyze fairly high in nutrients, compared to composted field weeds and leaves.

The nutrients in compost are held in desirable organic form. Whatever the fertility, it stays in the soil for a long time because humus particles break down slowly and release nutrients to plants over a very long period. Break-down is timed beautifully to coincide with plant demands. Losses from leaching are generally much lower than losses from equivalent quantities of inorganic fertilizers.

Compost particles mixed into soil aggregate it into crumbs and improve its texture. The particles themselves have an enormous capacity for storing water. In heavy soils compost improves soil's workability and allows water to penetrate better; in light, sandy soils, it works the other way, making them spongier and better able to retain moisture.

WHAT IS COMPOSTING?

Composting is probably as old as gardening. In its simplest form, all it amounts to is piling up refuse or throwing it into a pit, covering it with soil, and leaving it to decompose. Six months or a year later, you spade it back into the garden. The process is slow and space-consuming.

There are innumerable improvements on this procedure, of course. The first improvement is putting the debris in an enclosed bin where you can work with it easier. Some bins are shallow so low heat will enable earthworms to thrive in the compost mass. Others are tall, miniature silos, open at top and bottom. Some have solid masonry walls, and some are made of wire fencing. All a bin amounts to is a way of enclosing raw material while the microbes work on it. Each gardener supports his own method because it works for him. All these structures work; sooner or later, you are bound to get compost.

What actually takes place in the pile or bin is this: When you pile up mixed organic refuse and soak it down, you start a special kind of fire. Microbes in the trash proliferate in astronomical numbers. There are many individual kinds, but the aerobic or air-consuming microbes (these do most of the composting work) may be divided roughly into three classes:

High-heat bacteria go to work immediately and run the temperature of the pile up to 150-160° during the first few days. Given air, they produce heat enough to literally cook the organic material. They work mainly on soft, easily rotted ingredients that are high in protein.

Fungi appear in 7 to 10 days. Unable to tolerate the high heat in the center of the pile, they live in its outer shell—a zone 2 to 5 inches thick.

Actinomycetes, which show up last, are a race of bacteria distinct from those in the hot center of the pile. Like fungi they live in a zone of medium warmth near the pile's edges, and the two together give the material a grayish, cobwebby look. Both actinomycetes and fungi are extremely important in decomposition, since they successfully break down woody materials and even paper, which baffle high-heat bacteria near the pile's center.

The pile is a constantly changing thing. Microbe populations sweep up to dominate, then subside as the raw material they require is broken down into semi-composts, which, in turn, are grist for new populations succeeding them. Moisture and air are basic. Without moisture the process slows to a stop; without air anaerobic bacteria take over. They are not only foul smelling, but they are slow and inefficient as composting organisms.

Temperature at last begins to taper off, the pile assumes an earthy appearance, and the material becomes crumbly and ready for use.

From that point let's look at the recent developments.

1. What about the inoculums?

Some manufacturers claim compost "activators," enzymes, humic acid, bacterial cultures, additives, and inoculums add special strains of organisms to the compost pile. These organisms are supposed to hasten the break-down of the organic material. Manufacturers may state or imply that these products are essential to quick composting. Without exception, to our knowledge, unbiased scientific findings have shown that such claims are untrue.

In a number of carefully controlled tests, assorted compost activators, added to raw material in recommended amounts, have produced no observable effects. Those piles that were injected decomposed no faster than piles without activators.

The conclusion of these tests has been that all organisms necessary to the composting process are present from the beginning in raw untreated material. Even though a so-called activating product may be high in bacterial count, it contributes little or nothing to the result.

2. What has the University of California research revealed?

In 1951 scientists at the University of California set about to determine how *quickly* and *efficiently* compost could be made from raw waste. The study was prompted by concern over the depletion of organic matter in California soils and a growing interest in composting municipal garbage as a way of replenishing it. The project spanned two years and the report is a classic. (*Reclamation of Municipal Refuse by Composting,* Technical Bulletin 9, Sanitary Engineering Research Project, University of California, Berkeley; $1.) Many of the findings apply to home composters as well as to sanitary engineers.

Some of the findings suggest practices considerably different from what has always been standard composting procedure. The greatest conclusion was that neither soil nor manure is necessary to compost quickly and efficiently. Manure may hasten the process by supplying nitrogen if the bacteria in the raw mass need it. If they don't need it, nitrogen will be lost by dissipation as gas. Soil in the pile may actually slow down the composting process by interfering with the vital aeration.

The U. C. scientists were able to cut down

composting time from the typical 3 to 6 months to 12 days with ideal raw material, 14 days with average waste, and 21 days when material contained tough ingredients. Air, moisture, and the nature of raw material are the main critical factors.

3. What are the new methods?

The University of California method will probably change the idea of a compost bin somewhat, chiefly because more turning of the raw material will call for bins and receptacles that are easier to work in. A pile of organic refuse will eventually turn to compost no matter what you do. But turning green waste into usable compost in 3 weeks or less is a fine art. The Berkeley investigation pointed to these as critical factors in fast composting:

1. Proper mix of raw material.
2. Right texture or particle size.
3. Height of the pile.
4. Moisture.
5. Air supply.
6. Acidity-alkalinity (pH).

Let's take them up in that order:

Raw Material

The biological fire in a compost pile burns up carbon in the raw grist and uses the energy to turn the nitrogen it contains into protoplasm. An ideal compost material contains the two elements in the right proportions: just enough fuel units of carbon to convert each unit of nitrogen. The amount of carbon in the raw material, compared to the amount of nitrogen in it, is expressed as its carbon-nitrogen (C-N) ratio.

In general, tough, woody materials have high C-N ratios. Wheat straw, for example, has a C-N ratio of 197: it contains 197 parts of carbon for every part of nitrogen. Leafy, succulent materials have low C-N ratios. Examples: cabbage, 12; lawn clippings, 19; mixed border plants, 20 to 25.

If the C-N ratio of the raw mix is too high, it will take forever to break down. If it's too low, it will break down quite quickly, but a higher than normal proportion of leftover nitrogen will be wasted, being given off as ammonia gas. A C-N ratio of 30 is about right. This means that if you're composting tough material like ivy trimmings, woody weeds, and prunings, you should mix succulent material like lawn clippings and soft, leafy waste into the pile. An alternative, of course, is the conventional practice of adding nitrogen in the form of commercial fertilizer or manure.

Don't add fertilizer to a raw mix that has as low a C-N ratio as lawn clippings, green flower tops, and soft vegetable trimmings. Even without fertilizer the mix will lose nitrogen. What it needs is tougher refuse to raise its C-N ratio.

Texture, Particle size

Unless you can afford the luxury of a power compost grinder, your only control over particle size will be in choice of material for composting.

You can compost a hoe handle if you grind it fine enough and mix it with a nitrogen fertilizer to put its C-N ratio in order. Up to a point, the smaller the size of individual particles, the more surface is open to attack by microbes. However, limitations on fineness of grind are imposed by air requirements after the pile is formed. If you grind a material to fine consistency, it can settle solid.

A pile of lawn clippings will tend to sour and putrefy because it packs down tightly, and the middle of the pile lacks air. Mixed with coarser refuse and turned regularly, however, clippings break down in short order, since aerobic bacteria can work on them.

Pre-grinding trash allows you to compost all organic material in the garden, plus kitchen wastes as well—rose and fruit tree prunings, berry vines, pits, tough stalks, and leaves. But grinding should not be so fine as to cause pulping of succulent material. Ideal particles are about an inch in diameter.

Height and Heat

Heat build-up is all-important in composting, and one factor determining how high the temperature goes is the height of the pile. Too shallow a pile loses heat rapidly because there isn't enough material above the heat source to insulate it and prevent loss. Below-optimum temperatures mean that heat loving bacteria, working at the center of the pile, won't flourish as they should; therefore, composting will take a longer time. In addition, high temperatures, which are insurance against diseases, flies, and weeds, won't be sustained.

Too high a pile, on the other hand, means that material will be compressed by its own weight and there will be *too much* heat, plus a shortage of air at the bottom. Too much heat tends to kill off desirable bacteria and no air encourages the foul-smelling anærobic clan.

Experts arbitrarily set the height of the new compost pile at between 4 and 6 feet. A bin with walls 4 feet high may be filled 1 foot above the top to make a 5-foot pile, which is optimum. As decomposition progresses, the material will shrink in volume to perhaps 3 or 3½ feet.

In all but the most severe climates, outdoor air temperatures won't affect heat build-up in a pile of proper dimensions. Composting can be done in winter.

Moisture

While the pile should always be moist, it should never be soggy, since excess water

---

---

limits the air supply. The wetter it becomes, the more you'll have to turn it to keep aerobic bacteria flourishing.

Green refuse usually needs no additional water at all in the beginning. Dry stalks and grass should be wet down as the pile is built. Moisture of the pile as a whole should run between 40 and 60 per cent, which is about that of a squeezed sponge.

As heat begins to build, the pile will steam. It is apt to become dry at the center. If this happens, the process stops abruptly. The old method of inserting a pole in the pile, pulling it out occasionally to test heat and moisture, is a good one.

In dry climates the pile may need water every 4 or 5 days. But in areas where rainfall is heavy, you'll have to take precautions to keep the pile from becoming soggy. A rounded pile tends to shed water like a thatched roof, but if rains are continuous, a tarpaulin or similar covering over the bin is a better bet. When a pile has become water-logged, the anaerobes will take over quickly, but daily turning will put it back in healthy condition.

Air and Turning

The prime reason for turning compost is to put air into the center of the pile. Other reasons are placement of outside material in the hot center and adjusting moisture levels.

Turning is work, though it isn't too strenuous if you use a good manure fork and skim thin forkfuls off the top, taking your time. You can cut down the number of turnings required by using a bin with wide air cracks in its walls, by achieving the right degree of coarseness in the raw material, and by being careful not to get the pile too wet.

Wet material requires frequent turning, sometimes every day, until steaming gets rid of its sogginess. Your nose will tell you when the anaerobes are taking over, and when you get into the center of the pile, you'll see the characteristic pale green color. Turning will make it possible for the faster-working aerobic bacteria to function at the center of the pile again.

Drier material needs turning much less frequently. For maximum efficiency piles in the Berkeley tests were turned every 2 days if moisture was high and every 3 days if it was about right. Frequency of turning, we suspect, can be cut down considerably further in the home garden without loss of composting time.

Frequency of turning will depend on your schedule. If you're a weekend gardener, you'll turn it once a week. And if other elements are satisfactory, you'll get compost in short order.

Compost achieved by the 3-week method, even though well made, is apt to be pretty coarse. There will be stems and fibers in it, which make it awkward to handle.

Grass clippings can breed flies

What to do with grass clippings forever challenges those home owners who have: 1) a lawn, well fed and watered; 2) a reel lawn mower; 3) a grass-catcher attachment with which they choose to collect the clippings rather than let them lie on the grass.

If you have fed your lawn during the past month, and if you water it regularly, you are probably cutting a 1-inch grass crop off it every week. This makes a lot of clippings, especially if you have more than 1,000 square feet of lawn.

The best thing you can do with the clippings is compost them or spread them *in a thin layer* over the surface of garden beds to act as a moisture-holding, weed-checking mulch. The most impractical thing you can do with them is dump them in the garbage can—especially if your garbage can is barely adequate for the household garbage or if you pay for garbage collection on a weight or per-can basis. The worst thing you can do is pile the clippings in a big heap in the corner of your garden or put them in a box or barrel to take out to the dump one of these days.

WHY NOT PUT THE GRASS IN A PILE?

A three-foot pile of grass clippings appears to be harmless. The grass on the surface turns brown and the pile, representing several weeks' mowings, looks like a suburban version of a haystack. But it isn't. It breeds flies!

If you don't believe that a pile of grass can be a fly breeding place, stick a spade under the stack, turn it over and behold what's going on inside. We've done this; it is not a pretty sight at all.

In 1956 the Health Department of Santa Clara County, California (Division of Vector Control) issued a series of bulletins about sources of fly populations. Number 5 points at piled lawn clippings; this bulletin says that as many as 3,000 house fly larvae (maggots) have been found in a *single pint* sample of decomposing grass—perennial ryegrass, Kentucky blue, bent, clover, and other species.

The house fly was just one of four types of fly collected as larvae from piled lawn clippings. The county men also collected false stable fly, soldier fly, and the lesser house fly. The lesser house fly is the little one that flies around and around in the middle of the living room or beneath the patio overhead and seldom alights. The regular house fly rests on the table, flies a little, and then rests some more.

It doesn't take long for flies to develop in piled grass. Adult flies can emerge from a breeding place in as little as six days after the eggs were laid. And this can happen in grass clippings piled only two inches deep.

At the bottom of a pile of grass clippings a week old, or older, you will also discover that the grass has turned into a slimy, yellowish-brown, odorous mass. It does this because it has a high water content when cut, and the clippings, piled flat together, leave little or no room for air.

High water content plus low air content encourage development of anaerobic bacteria. They are the smell-producing bacteria. The opposite faction, the aerobic bacteria, work where air is present and bring about decomposition just as fast, or faster, without producing bad odors. Aerobic bacteria are the ones that work for you breaking down vegetable material in a properly functioning compost pile.

CAREFUL COMPOSTING IS ALL RIGHT

Naturally, if you pile three or four basket loads of clippings on top of your compost pile and just leave them there, you get just what you get from a grass pile in a corner—flies and bad smells. But if you turn the clippings frequently (every two or three days) and water after each turning, the anaerobic bacteria will never get a real foothold. Decomposition will take place fast, courtesy of aerobic bacteria. In a short time, you will get a clean, nutrient-rich compost from your clippings.

Or you may throw the clippings on the pile in alternate thin layers with leaves, plant tops, or weeds. Or you may mix the rough vegetation with the clippings. Either method insures air spaces and lessens the chance for anaerobic stagnation.

SPREAD CLIPPINGS THIN AS A MULCH

If you have several large beds of shrubs, dahlias, roses, camellias, strawberries, or anything that doesn't cover the ground completely, you might spread the grass clippings over the soil beneath them. The grass will check water evaporation from the surface and discourage weed growth to a degree. Each week, spread the clippings on another bed. If, at this rate, you can work your way back to the original bed in two or three weeks, the original bed will then be ready for another mulching. A thin layer of grass clippings (no deeper than one inch) dries up in a short time and almost disappears.

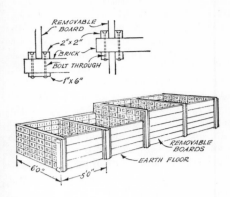

Concrete block *compost bins have good air circulation, which hastens decomposition. End bins are smaller as compost packs down, takes less space. Boards in front slide between strips bolted to the blocks*

Four ideas for compost bins

WILLIAM APLIN

Bin shown below and left, built by Martin Schaffer of Alhambra, California, combines compactness and accessibility. The center boards are removable, making it possible to change the bin from a two chamber to a one chamber container. The advantage of a two chamber bin is that, periodically, you can turn the compost from one side to another, thereby expos-

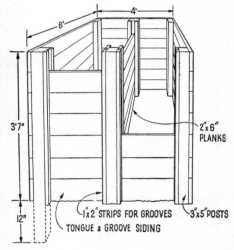

ing on top the older, well-rotted compost. As the compost is used, the front slats can be removed one at a time.

Placed over the top of the heap at left is a damp gunny sack to keep flies off the compost and to prevent the pile from drying out. It's made from two potato sacks stitched end to end. A piece of ½-inch pipe is sewn into one end to make covers easier to toss over the pile.

Structure above *has three bins: One is for storing new material, another is for matter being cured, and the third is for the com-* *post that is cured and ready for use. Each bin is a 4-foot cube, with removable 1 by 6-inch slats for easy access to the compost*

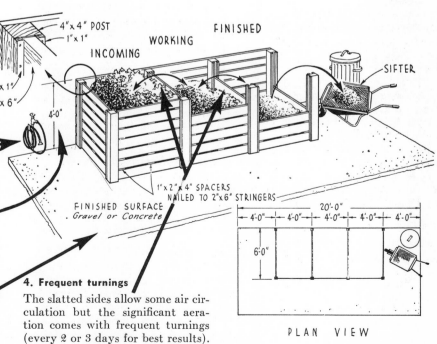

This compost receptacle illustrates physical features that help make fast compost without aid of soil or manure. Many bins and boxes now in existence can be worked by this method.

1. Water always handy

Hose and sprinkler supply water that keeps fast-working compost damp as a squeezed sponge.

2. Optimum height 4 to 6 feet

If a pile is too low, heat is lost rapidly and composting action slows. If too high, the weight will compress the material, cut off vital air and make too much heat.

3. Place to handle raw material

Material should be walnut-size chunks or smaller. Space allows for temporary stacking to await any necessary grinding, chopping.

4. Frequent turnings

The slatted sides allow some air circulation but the significant aeration comes with frequent turnings (every 2 or 3 days for best results). This set of bins designed for easiest possible access with manure fork.

4″ x 4″ POST
1″ x 1″
INCOMING WORKING FINISHED
SIFTER
1″ x 1″
2″ x 6″
4′-0″
1″ x 2″ x 4″ SPACERS
NAILED TO 2″x6″ STRINGERS
FINISHED SURFACE
Gravel or Concrete

20′-0″
4′-0″ 4′-0″ 4′-0″ 4′-0″ 4′-0″
6′-0″

PLAN VIEW

The 4-foot width gives room for wheelbarrow and manure fork.

The materials you work with

As the pages of this book prove, you have a wide choice of materials to choose from. Which should you use? Your choice, of course, will depend upon many factors other than the material itself. However, here are a few facts that may help you.

LATH

The standard lath size is ⅜ by 1½ inches wide and comes in 4, 6, and 8-foot lengths. Many builders prefer to use 1 by 2-inch lumber to avoid the warping and sagging that is normal with lath.

The amount of shade is controlled by the spacing. While a more or less standard method is to space the width of one lath apart, many growers place them closer for ferns, tuberous begonias, fuchsias, but wider apart for azaleas, rhododendrons, and other part shade plants.

Aluminum lath is available and its method of application using aluminum stringers, clips, etc., has been carefully worked out by the manufacturers.

Aluminum is also used as slats fastened to wood frames. Built as framed panels, these slats make light weight shades that can be placed over the glass of the greenhouse for summer shade, and removed and stored away in fall and winter.

SARAN SHADE CLOTH

Applications of this material can be seen on pages 62 to 65. This pliable plastic screen is woven in meshes of various sizes. You can specify the percentage of shade you want—72 per cent, 63 per cent, 55 per cent, 51 per cent, 47 per cent, 30 per cent. The 51 per cent mesh gives about the same light as lath, placed a lath width apart. However, the light is diffused rather than in a pattern as with lath.

Saran is dark green in color. Cost is about 4 to 7 cents a square foot depending on mesh, binding, and quantity. Life expectancy is about 10 years.

This fabric is manufactured in widths from 6 feet to 20 feet, in lengths up to 900 feet. In some localities this shade cloth is available in prepared sizes—12 by 12, 12 by 18, and 12 by 24 with reinforced edging and grommets so that overhead may be laced in place. It is possible to order special sizes for an additional charge.

This material can substitute for lath over a standard post and beam construction or can be supported by galvanized wire strung between posts. Cloth can be fastened to wire with hog rings or laced to wire with saran thread.

PLASTIC FILMS

Plastic films are widely used by plant growers to get inexpensive "greenhouse" space. The light weight films are inexpensive enough to make yearly renewal practical. The more sunlight and the more intense the sunlight the faster the plastic deteriorates. Around the home garden it should be used where a temporary shelter is needed. One of the most satisfactory uses is film over a lath shelter. Lath gives it the support it needs to prevent wind damage.

Manufacturers are doing their best to bring out a plastic film that will stand up over a long period of time in all climates. Some success has been obtained in climates with low light intensities but not in such areas as Arizona and inland California.

WOVEN REED SCREENS

Reeds woven with stainless steel wire are available in rolls 6 feet, 4 inches high, by 25 feet long. It costs about $15 a roll, or 10 cents a square foot. You see this material in use on pages 22, 23, and 44. This inexpensive material shows signs of wear by peeling and fading almost immediately but most home owners find it pleasant to live with even after four or five years of use.

WOVEN SPLIT BAMBOO

This material is available in rolls similar to the reed screen. There are two grades, one with light, and one with heavy pieces of bamboo. Both are more substantial than reed screen, last longer, cost more. This screening, too, may give too much shade but like the reed screen, it is very useful and decorative as a wind screen.

METAL LOUVER SCREENS

There are a number of metal louvered screens all built on the principle of slanting tiny louvers at an angle to intercept the sun but provide light. They are used as summer covers for greenhouses.

WINDOW OR INSECT SCREENING

Regular window screening, both metal and glass fiber, cannot be considered as shade giving materials. However, their value in keeping out insects and reducing wind movement is important.

GLASS FIBER CLOTH

Glass fiber shading cloth is just coming onto the market and is not widely available. One greenhouse manufacturer makes this cloth available as rolled up shades to fit various sized greenhouses.

Glass fiber cloth breaks up direct sunlight, gives a more even shade than the full light-full dark pattern of slat shades.

GLASS FIBER-REINFORCED PLASTIC PANELS

Reinforced plastic panels should not be thought of as shading materials. Although the panels cut out some of the sun's rays, some colors of this material seem to collect light and most trap heat beneath it. In climates where cool days outnumber the warm ones, plastic panels are used in overheads of all types as a substitute for glass. Greenhouse manufacturers recommend reinforced plastic panels in areas where hail storms are hazards.

Both corrugated and flat plastic panels come in these sizes:

26-inch wide (for rafters 24 inches on center); 33-inch wide (for rafters 30 inches on center); 40-inch wide (for rafters 36 inches on center); and other widths up to 4 feet. Lengths are: 8, 10, 12 feet long. A supporting framework for plastic panels needs cross blocking between rafters for rigidity. This should be at a minimum interval of 4 feet for 26-inch-wide panels, 3 feet 6 inches for 33-inch panels, and 3 feet for 40-inch panels.

OTHER PANELS

Plywood panels are used in several ways. To give a lath type shade, ¼-inch exterior grade plywood is sawed lengthwise (except 4 inches at either end of panel) at 2-inch intervals, then sprung for strength and pattern with a 2 by 6-inch spacer.

For exterior use (roofs, walls) there's an exterior grade Douglas fir plywood with a resin impregnated fiber bonded to both sides. (See work center, pages 62 to 65.) Corrugated aluminum panels, now available in colors, are being much used in overheads. The combination of aluminum panels and reinforced plastic panels gives a quick and easy way to bring overhead light into a structure. The light and heat reflecting qualities of the aluminum tend to balance the heat input of the plastic.

Another solid panel for outdoor use is asbestos cement board. This is available in ⅛ and 3/16-inch thicknesses, and in panels up to 5 by 9 feet.

GLASS

As is evident in many examples throughout the book, glass is the old standby among overhead materials and should not be overlooked or underrated.

RECOMMENDED READING

The *Sunset* book, *How to Build Patio Roofs*, contains further information on many of the materials discussed here, with many illustrated examples. It makes an excellent companion piece to this book.